Anna Carlisle, originally from Melbourne, Australia, is presently a local writer, editor and English teacher who successfully combines her outdoor passions with her cerebral and literary pursuits.

She co-authored *Introducing Shakespeare* (OUP 1994) while still a teacher in Melbourne and she has an Australian novel and a play regarding the Aboriginal peoples currently in progress. Otherwise known as Angie Cairns, she has lived in the UK for the past ten years, both in London and presently half-way up a hill in Hebden Bridge.

Published 2004 by Pennine Pens

ISBN 1 873378 18 1

Published by Pennine Pens.
32, Windsor Road, Hebden Bridge,
West Yorkshire, HX7 8LF.
Tel 01422-843724
books@penninepens.co.uk
www.hebdenbridge.co.uk
www.penninepens.co.uk

GONE WALKABOUT

Pennine Pens

For my father

CONTENTS

ILLUSTRATIONS

ACKNOWLEDGEMENTS

The walks in this book began life as monthly contributions to *The Hebden Bridge Times* and *Todmorden News*, and I acknowledge with gratitude the willingness of Sheila Tordoff, the Editor, both to initiate and continue the three series of walks which were subsequently featured in the papers.

Chris Ratctiffe at Pennine Pens expressed almost immediate willingness to publish the walks in book form and I thank him for all his quiet and masterly work in producing this elegant little edition.

My thanks to those who have spurred me on to record - as a 'blow in' (or 'Offcumden') to the area - my heady experiences of Pennine West Yorkshire on foot and who have been great sources of inspiration in themselves: in particular, to Kerry McQuade and Jill Liddington, as 'colleagues' and mentors, I say a heartfelt thank you.

And, of course, my firmest encourager, backer and inspirer, who believes implicitly and eternally - it would seem - in my abilities: Alexandra Mathie.

CLOSER TO HOME

12 WALKS DESIGNED TO BEGIN
AND END IN HEBDEN BRIDGE

Commute to a city and feel that all you know of your own valley is the A646, the Co-Op and the Crown Street chippie? Want some relief from the symptoms of the dreaded British virus, DIY? Do you dream of the sharp Pennine air cutting artistically into your cheeks and making them into year-round peaches?

Then these first twelve walks are for you.

And what about those headaches? Sleeplessness? Poor digestion? Let me help you with those too. This little book is a guide to physical health and spiritual awakening: helping you to fall in love with your environs all over again by courting them on foot and by walking your own Pennine way to fitness. You can talk to the trees and the cows and the sheep and not consider yourself a nutcase. You will want to sing, yodel or scream your exhilaration from the hilltops. You will marvel anew at the joys of living in the Calder Valley.

These walks were initially published monthly in the *Hebden Bridge*

Times and *Todmorden News* weekly newspapers, and these first twelve – Closer to Home — are designed for those who live in or close to the heart of Calderdale: Hebden Bridge. They are nonetheless accessible to all Calderdale – and many greater Yorkshire – dwellers. Hebden Bridgers should aim to keep the car where they left it on Friday night and set off and return to their own front door. Out-of-towners may drive, or take the bus or train, to the starting points. These first walks will take you no further than seven or eight miles at the most. They are tailored to the fit, the moderately fit and the distinctly unfit; simply adjust the timescale and the shortcuts to your own abilities. But given where we live, you won't be surprised, I'm sure, if the walks go up a lot?

You'll need to be lissom enough, I guess, to shinny up the many slippery mule-tracks which ribbon our valley and which require either strong-ish ankles or a tractor-tread on your boots. (Leave trainers – which will only slip and sully – at home with your woes.) Apart from these, you will require only a thigh-length waterproof and perhaps a stick for those of you who will find the uneven terrain a challenge. It's generally preferable to keep your hands free of clutter; you may need them to lever you up moss-covered staircases or down a sudden rocky beck. In your pockets, have this book, the house keys, a mobile and a pocketful of quenching money (as homely hostelries are built into the walks, usually at their finishing lines – otherwise you may never finish at all!)

These are all-weather walks. Many can be squeezed in at the end of a summer's working day while others will need to be left until the weekend offers three or four hours of straight daylight. But take courage in foul weather: if you are kitted out warm and dry, then the deepest January snows and the freezing gales of February will be bracing. Remember that your local hills are always – except perhaps when they are invisible and it is permissible to stay indoors – always breathtakingly beautiful.

Without going to extremes, it could be said that these are walks for all ages, as long as an adult is in attendance. Most mobile elderly folk could manage at least part of all of these walks. No young child, I believe, should be far from home without an adult; and a dog is a wise companion for any solo walker.

Over the next twelve walks, I shall be training you to take off safely on your own or in small groups, and to savour the historical, botanical and topographical delights of our valley. The walks are 'circular': there is no greater disincentive to keeping up the walking habit than sameness; no one much wants to see the same territory twice, certainly not on the same day. Circular walks bring you home to the familiar by travelling the unknown. Each will offer new vistas. After the twelfth walk, I hope you feel you could start the whole series over again and still feel the delight of novelty – or even of nostalgia. Or better still, walk the whole twelve routes in reverse – same territory only curiously different when viewed backwards, especially after a little time has elapsed.

Whichever way you do the walks, I dare you to tire of them. They should keep you entranced for months. Your armchair lethargy will miraculously disappear at each step; aches and pains will melt into the dew; and a surge of good health will buzz around your body. May you love walking around the Calder Valley so much that it becomes an integral part of your new life, something always worth turning the telly off for. Delights beyond words and beauty you never saw from the car on the valley floor are waiting to make you feel very, very special.

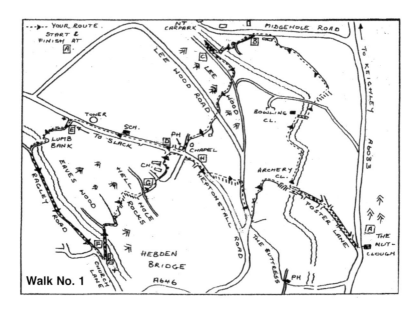

Walk No. 1

WALK NO. 1

HEPTONSTALL, HELL HOLE
AND HOME TO HEBDEN

*The Nutclough (GR995275) – Midgehole – Heptonstall – Lumb Bank -
Hell Hole rocks –* **Hebden Bridge town centre.**

Distance: 4.4 miles (7 km). With stops, leave 2-3 hours
Conditions: Some steep sections, a couple of slippery
                 descents
Level: Easy - medium

Right? Everybody ready? Got the dog on a lead and the children
buttoned up? Got money and the keys and a mobile and not a lot else
to clutter you up on this relatively short walk? Check your boots and
make sure they'll be reliable friends on the unstraight and narrow.
Make sure your trousers are loose and comfortable – not denim, for
example; it will stick to you like clay if the rain sets in. Done? Good!
Well then, let's set off.

A   **Start at the Nutclough** (where the old Nutclough House
hotel used to be) and set off down Foster Lane to its end. Cross the
tiny hump-back bridge over Hebden Water and turn right onto the
river path, signposted to Hardcastle Crags. With the Archery Club on
your left, follow this pretty path round a most picturesque bend in the
river and cross the river by the bridge at the Bowling Club. Take in the
impressive 'falls' in the river on your left. The path soon crosses a
gravelled lower stretch of Lee Mill Road; go up some deep, steep
steps and then turn left onto the path to take you onto the tarmaced
Midgehole Road.

B   **Head along Midgehole Road** for a mere 300 metres until you
reach the clump of cottages and the horse field close to the Dying and
Finishing Works. Take the farm-track down on your left; once past the
attractive stone farmhouse on your right, go through the little
wooden gate in the wall and cross the field towards the river once

13

more – taking care to secure both gates after you. Cross the bridge and follow the path for 100 metres until you come to a signpost pointing your way uphill; turn sharp left, almost going back on yourself, onto the cobbled mule-path – now part of the Calderdale Way. The cobbles are worn down into a rugged but slippery surface, so watch your step on this section.

C **Cross the tarmaced sliproad from Lee Wood Road to Hebden Hey,** then continue up the hill, still on the cobbles. Take your time and enjoy working your thighs on such thoroughly uneven ground, but be alert to the approaching Lee Wood Road – which is always busy with traffic. Again, cross the road when it is clear and continue on the unmade track up past the 'junction' with imposing North Well House, bearing right here. Past the house, stop at the low wall and take in the quite staggering views of Hebden Bridge and the valley to the east. Then amble on up into the historic back lanes of Heptonstall. (Add an extra hour or so to your journey-time if you wish to stop and appreciate the octagonal chapel where John Wesley once preached, or St Thomas' church and its sixteenth-century ruins, the grave of Sylvia Plath or the local museum.)

D **Walk out of Heptonstall by heading up the cobbled high street (west)** past the primary school on your right and, a little further on, past a horse field on your left, to the Lumb Back 'junction' – where on a grassy mound you can sit on a thoughtful bench and absorb the almost 360 degrees of views, spectacular in any weather: over to Stoodley Pike in the south, Colden and Widdop to the west, and north to Haworth Moor.

E **Follow the lane south to Lumb Bank** – when you have drunk your fill of the air and the unbroken beauty at the top – staying on the tarmac till the lane's end and resisting the temptation to turn left at the bottom and hole up for the rest of the week in the inspiring sur-roundings of the Arvon Foundation; I'm sure you'll already feel like an inspired poet by this stage of your walk, but Arvon only takes the pre-booked. Walk straight ahead off the tarmac and carefully pick your way down the rough path to the river (Colden Water this time) and arrive at a delightful stone bridge where white water tumbles loud and furious over rocks and where the chimney of the defunct Lower Lumb mill pokes its head through the trees. Continue on and join Ragley Lane (the route between Mytholm and Jacks Bridge), a fairly rough and bepuddled track which joins Church Lane at its bottom.

(**Conversely, you can turn off Lumb Lane at the back wall of Lumb Bank,** passing the extremely pretty wardens' cottage on your left, and follow the wooded glade path down – beneath Hell Hole Rocks – with soft leaf-mould underfoot and great umbrellas of oak branches overhead – down through Eaves Wood to the steps cut into the bank which will take you uphill once again. This is a slightly shorter - and even more beautiful - route down the hill, especially since you have another stiff climb ahead.)

F **(Turn left onto Eaves Road,** behind St James' Church and Hebden Royd School, cross the bridge and then take the track first on your right; this is 'Church View' which leads you around to the left and onto the attractive leafy path where your short-cutting friends might now meet you!) You are now between Eaves Wood and Granny Wood, where a stepped path cut into the bank will lead you up, up and up the Hell Hole rockface: the steps are deep and steep but manageable at a steady pace. When you reach the top, stop for breath and gaze thankfully over to Horsehold and Stoodley and down the valley towards Todmorden. Again, you should feel richly rewarded for your efforts – what a marvellous climb!

G **Turn towards the village,** taking the walled path between the newer houses and you will reach the rear of St Thomas' Church. Either traverse the churchyard (but you may have visited it earlier on the walk) or pick your way through the ancient alley of West Laithe to meet the high street of Heptonstall once again. You are now ready for the last leg of your journey and the leisurely descent into Hebden Bridge.

H **Walk down the road from Heptonstall towards Hebden Bridge, turning left at the footpath signpost** and taking the stone staircase down to Lee Wood Road. (Beware as you step onto the road as traffic hurtles fast around this blind bend.) Cross the road and turn left onto the cobbled path of Slater Bank which forks right a little way down, and winds you down once more to Foster Lane. Take your time on the slippery cobbles (the handrail will help keep you vertical) and have a chat to the three benign cows in the field on your right. Arrive back at the hump-back bridge onto Foster Lane, and head either via Victoria Road or the Keighley Road towards the White Lion hotel - or one of the town's fine coffee shops - for some well-earned refreshments.

Pleasantly tired or completely exhilarated? Calf muscles pulsating or your corns really playing up? Don't worry; not only will you recover in no time and get a great sleep tonight, but I bet you'll be itching for the next in the series when the beauty of today's walk will be symmetried on the other side of the A646 when you tackle the dizzying heights of Wood Top and Horsehold. Cheers!

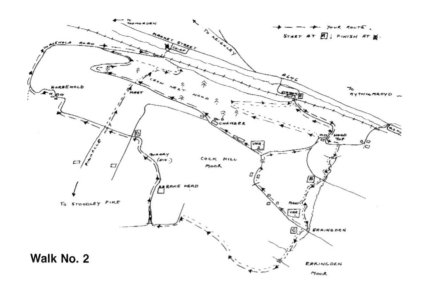

Walk No. 2

17

WALK NO. 2

BLOW AWAY YOUR BLUES ABOVE WOOD TOP

*Hebden Bridge Station (GR995268) – Wood Top - Cock Hill Moor
- Rake Head - Horsehold - Hebden Bridge*

Distance: 3.5 miles (5.5 km). With stops, leave 2 hours
Conditions: Some steep sections, and a section of bog
Level: Easy - medium

This is an enchanting walk, taking you into country south of the A646 where, if you pick a nice clear day, the beauty of Erringden Moor and Stoodley Pike will blow you over - and so might the wind. This is one of those walks that will make you feel privileged to be alive and living in the Calder Valley.

You will note that at the head of each walk, I am building in a grid reference; should you wish to refer to something slightly more precise than my own maps, then have OS Outdoor Leisure map 21 (South Pennines) with you as well. And if you walk alone, as I often do, it is smart thinking to carry a whistle around your neck and - that amazing boon to walkers' safety - a mobile phone in your pocket. You never know when you may slip and twist something or fall and break something, or simply feel unsafe and in need of the human voice. I shall rarely be taking you so far from civilisation in this series that loud blasts on a whistle would not be heard at a farmhouse or by other walkers, or that you can't get a mobile signal, so, even if you never need them, they can be comforting companions.

A   **At Hebden Bridge Station**, come out of the booking office and turn right down to the track which goes under the railway bridge. From there walk up the very rough track until it meets the Wood Top road (just after Palace House Road on the right). Climb up this now concrete road until you reach Wood Top, but bear left onto rough track once again, just before the houses on your right. Follow the track around until you see a signpost at the stone wall on your right, directing you south across a field and into woods. Then pick your way over a stream via a slate slab and follow the track uphill through the trees - keeping the stream on your left and a field on your right. The track will come to an end at the Wood Top road (which soon becomes Park Lane to Mytholmroyd) which has come around to meet you.

B   Cross the Wood Top road where the footpath, signposted to Wood Hey Clough, will resume. The path up the hill from this point becomes progressively steep but it is very grassy and pleasant walking. It takes you uphill on smooth ground for a good half-mile through bramble, birch trees and bracken. Pass under power lines near a pylon on the right of the path, zigzagging a little as you reach the top, and you will reach the Erringden road at a stile. This is another rough track. Turn right onto it so that you are now facing west.

C   (**After this point**, the walk becomes more difficult, and a boggy section awaits you. If you feel that such terrain is not a match for your ankles or that you don't need any more hill, then go to *Variation 1 or **2 and take a less strenuous - but quite bracing and beautiful - return walk to town.)

Facing west now, turn almost immediately left off the Erringden road at a PF signpost. The path will take you up, beside a rocky 'ditch' and across a small stream, to a stile. You are now facing Cock Hill Moor - the western end of Erringden Moor - and, for the next quarter of a mile, you are more or less on your own. The thin line of path will become difficult to discern, but never fear if you lose it altogether. Basically, concentrate on heading southwest up the hill and on placing your feet firmly on safe, dry tussocks. If you also keep the occasional eye out for the crest of the hill, you will see the two black chimneys of Rake Head farmhouse come into view. Head for the farmhouse, but hastening slowly over the bog, of course.

When you reach the farm wall with its deterring barbed-wire trim, turn left and, with the wall to your right, follow it around a corner - not forgetting to stop for at least a moment and take in the truly glorious views over Erringden Moor, Spring Wood and Bell House Moor and beyond - until you come to a farm gate. Turn right here and you will find yourself walking down an 'avenue' of wall towards Rake Head farmhouse, surely the most solitary-looking farmhouse in the locale but with the most imposing proportions - and the most spectacular views. If you skitter in to a small disused quarry below the farmhouse, you will get a great panorama of the valley and all the hills and moors to the north, even as far beyond as Haworth Moor. Continue then down the hill until you reach the tarmac of upper Horsehold Road and an equally stunning set of views - over to Lumbutts on one hand and Blackshaw Head on the other - opens out in front of you.

D **Head straight down towards Horsehold**, soaking up the pleasure of the attractive fields before you and the spectrum of Stoodley Pike, Heptonstall and Mount Skip around you. The wind will buffet your cheeks and beg to come in under your jacket. Breathe deep and feel wonderful. You may only regret that you are now on the downhill path and that the main challenge of your walk is behind you. As the road descends, you will cross the Pinnacle Way, remembering that this route to Stoodley Pike awaits you on another day. Stop here and choose: you can either 1) stay on the road and wind down through the tiny hamlet of Horsehold, or 2) go through the gate on your right and head off north across the field, over a farm track and into Crow Nest Wood. Clamber carefully down through the leaf-mould floor of the wood until you come out of the trees and you can clearly see the path down to Fairfield and Palace House Road back into town.

If you 1) stay on the Horsehold Road, you will be rewarded by fields full of sheep and cows, a paddockful of chickens and the rustic handful of Horsehold houses. Wind down beyond the cobbles of Horsehold Road and saunter on down into town, hitting civilisation at Market Street.

For either route-taker, coffee shops and pubs aplenty await you in the centre of Hebden Bridge.

*Variation 1: Don't feel hard done by! You may miss the breath-taking crest of the hill, but you will be handsomely compensated by the views over to Midgley and Warley and beyond. Follow the Erringden road down, past a cluster of farmhouses, to the 'junction' with the Old Chamber road. Bear right down the hill, following the cobbled, then tarmaced road down to Wood Top. Where you meet the houses, turn left beyond the Royal Mail post-box in the wall and you will find yourself in the glorious glades of Crow Nest Wood, as pretty as a picture, which will lead you gently down to Fairfield and Palace

House Road and back into town.

Variation 2:   As above, until the Old Chamber 'junction' where, instead of bearing right, turn left onto this track, past two groups of newly restored farmhouses on your right until, at Old Chamber, the track forks. Veer right and follow the track down for about three-quarters of a mile (with Crow Nest Wood staying on your right) until you meet the tarmac of lower Horsehold Road.

Join the road by turning right and head back down to Market Street.

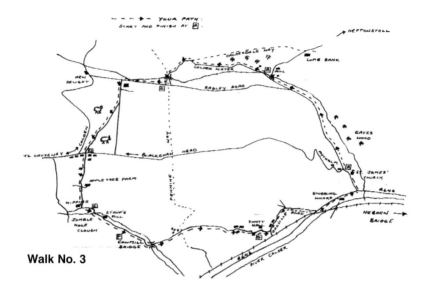

Walk No. 3

WALK NO. 3:

A JUMBLED WEALTH OF HISTORY AND SCENERY

*St James' Church (GR984274) - Lumb Bank - Jacks Bridge
- Hippins - Jumble Hole Clough - Hebden Bridge*

Distance: 5 miles (8 km). Leave 3 hours
Conditions: Slippery as a rule in wooded and river sections.
                  Steep (up and down) at times
Level: Medium

This walk has ghostly beauty. It hems you in to valleys where industry has stood still but where vital rivers still throb and thunder - and stun you with their deafening, insistent therapy. It floors you with the grandeur of the once-thriving mills; it takes you past four or five mill-skeletons which seem so curiously alive: they still seem to be growing out of the clough walls, subtly clothed in moss and leaves and evoking haunting images for us. You can almost hear, over the water's drone, the clacking of clogs on the cobbled steps and the whinnying of the laden mules that laboured daily up and down these cloughs. You'll be staggered by the scenery and the history, and will feel richer indeed when you stumble back home from Jumble Hole.

Have your camera with you as well this time. You never know what ghostly, unearthly beauties you might want to capture.

A   From St James' Church, head up Church Lane and take the second turn on the right, Ragley Lane (the old Colden Road) towards Jack's Bridge. After about half a mile of this pot-holed track, and ignoring the fork up to the left, peel off right onto the lower track, as far as the little stone bridge set over Colden Water and the imperious chimney of Lower Lumb Mill.

B   Just before the bridge, turn left and pass around a metal gate, taking the path up to the left of Colden Water. The walk becomes immediately thrilling as you skirt the water pulsating and pounding over the rocks. Soon you will find that you have - perhaps unwittingly - crossed the river: a platformed culvert, very 'earthed' over, takes you now into magical Colden Clough where the glorious wall of Higher Lumb Mill stands commandingly before you. Cross over a second, smaller culvert, and up stone steps until you reach the 'parapet' wall of the mill, and saunter (carefully) along it. You have been staying as close as possible to the river-bank, but now start bearing right and upwards, heading to a high clearing where your path is joined by the main upper path from Bob Wood. Follow the path onto yet another mill-race wall, which soon takes you down again to river level. Ahead of you is the brilliantly constructed stone footbridge: Hebble Hole bridge, a very pretty stopping-place. Then take the right-hand path beyond the bridge, up the steep hill onto the top end of Ragley Road (Hudson Mill Road at this point).

C   Turn right onto Hudson Mill Road, hitting the tarmac after a quarter of mile, and turning left past the farmhouse on your left. Just past the house, the path takes you up a walled footpath and straight (south) up the hill. (You are closely parallel to the Pennine Way, only a matter of metres to the east.) Once on this rocky path, a slatted gate in the wall on your right will put you onto the Calderdale Way; set off across the fields - about three or four of them to be shared respectfully with the sheep - and emerge onto the road just before the Blackshaw Head junction.

D   Cross the road here and pass through a group of houses just before the junction with the Colden-Long Causeway road. A signpost guides your way, but the path is mostly walled and paved and easy to follow at this stage. Cling close to the farmhouses until you pass Apple Tree Farm on your left. You are now on the path down to Hippins, a very handsome seventeenth-century farmhouse. Here turn left at the CW Link Path and you will enter a usually wet field, flooded by infant streams, which will slow down your hitherto steady pace. Bear with it and soon another signpost will point you south down the hill into Jumble Hole Clough, where further aqueous and historic delights await you.

E   A stepped path leads you down into Jumble Hole Clough and across a picturesque footbridge. It then takes you onto the high wall of Staup's Mill - and a mystical atmosphere immediately envelopes you as you approach this gaunt ruin. Since the walls and window-areas still remain, it is easy to picture the productivity that droned on here a hundred years ago. There is a spectacular waterfall which tumbles down from the clough wall on your left and the camera will be begging for action. It is a crumbly old place, however, so do take care where you put your feet.

As soon as you can tear yourself away, rejoin the footpath up to the right, then take a left and continue down the clough. On your left, the water crashes down at break-neck speed, thundering over rocks in its path and disregarding all obstacles, whilst we have to pick our way more carefully. There's a chastening lesson in the water for all of us - perhaps the way we'd like to get on in life, but mayn't.

F   The precipitous path down the clough soon becomes gentler and leads you, past Cow Bridge Mill pond on your left, then to Cow Bridge itself, where cars are often parked and your first reminder for some time of modern life. Take a look at the pretty ruins of Spa Mill with its curved, moss-covered retaining walls, but then return to the bridge and peel off left, up the hill. You will pass a tiny cemetery containing a heart-stopping number of infant graves: a poignant place. The Pennine Way weaves its way behind the graveyard; ignore it and carry on in an easterly direction over the crest of the hill, then down past Higher Underbank House and onto a smaller path, passing intrusively close to farmhouses such as Knott Hall.

G   After Knott Hall, join a road just north of the railway line, and go left before the arch into Stoney Lane. Head uphill, and then veer right into Oakville Road. Where this road meets the A646, start heading towards Hebden Bridge - or for another 250 yards at least: as you are now close to your finishing point, I think a stoup or two at the Stubbing Wharf hostelry may be in order. When well-watered, carry on to Bankfoot, finishing with a left turn into Church Lane, and be proud of your own - and others' - labours. You have traversed some beautifully unspoiled terrain and seen treasures aplenty en route. Perhaps there's someone we can thank?

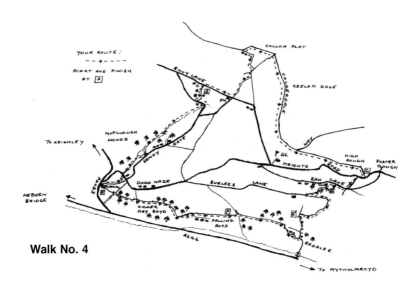

Walk No. 4

WALK NO. 4

RICH AND VARIED ROUTE TO REDACRE

Stubbings School (GR994274) - Nutclough Woods - Collom Flat -
Redacre Wood - Fallingroyd - **Hebden Bridge**

Distance: 5 miles (8 km). Leave 3 hours
Conditions: Clear paths, but sometimes wet and slippery.
A steep descent and some traversing of sloping
terrain
Level: Easy - medium

Woods and clough, close and cosy fields, rugged moorland and quite
a lot of water: this is a walk that offers a bit of everything. And yet it's
not overly demanding. It's ideal for a breath of good air after a
Sunday lunch; it'll burn the calories off and the pudding up. If you'll
just get off that sofa and bring that lump of tiredness with you, I guar-
antee that within fifteen minutes of the Great Calderdale Outdoors it
will have vanished.

Much of this walk, it must be said, is slippery, slopey and uneven
- so you'll need to take the usual care. But remember to look up from
your feet every now and then to take in the falls and the dells and the
far-flung views.

A   **Facing Stubbings School, walk up the cobbled snicket**
called Bank Side. Just before the top, turn first path left into
Alexandra Road. At the end of the rows of houses, you will be on
Birchcliffe Road, facing both Chapel Avenue and the Birchcliffe
Centre, formerly one of the grandest Baptist chapels in the valley.

Cross over into Chapel Avenue and at its end you will enter the
Nutclough Woods. Now as a vintage Birchcliffean, I may be a little
biased, but I'd say you are now entering one of the loveliest parts of
Heavenly Bridge, much though the woods might presently be in need
of some care and attention. Pick your way carefully over the rough,
sloping path between handsome tall trees, and you will find yourself
at the peaceful 'pond' that is the legacy of the old mill; it is at the time
of writing quite badly silted up and in need of some regeneration; it is

home to only a couple of ducks now and the water has virtually halted in its fall from the nearby clough, but be assured that there are groups of concerned local citizens who are keen to work for its renaissance.

Cross the pond at some stepping-stones at the foot of the clough and make your way up the high path that leads you up, up to the arched stone bridge and then up again to the beautiful beck of Ibbotroyd. In the summer I like to park my whole self in the water here, if I can tolerate its perennial coldness; it is such a restorative little place. Continue up the winding, now rather difficult path until you come to Walker Lane. Cross the road here and take the path up beside the new houses at Chiserley until you reach Billy Lane, with the Post Office to your left and the school to your right.

B   Turn right onto Billy Lane and follow the road as far as the Hare and Hounds on your right. Turn left at this 'junction' and make your way, bearing left, towards Commons Farm. Behind the farmhouse where the straw-bale bathroom stands removed and alone, take a gate out of farm territory and onto the Calderdale Way at Collon Flat. Now turn east and follow the CW Way past Keelam Edge and Cock Hill (above Hebden Bridge Golf Club) and stride along the ridge on firm, safe ground. This is your longest stretch of open country and, should the day be clear, the views afforded will be just gorgeous, especially over to our familiar south and west: Heptonstall and Stoodley directions respectively, and even as far east as Norlands Moor. Past Cock Hill, keep to the lower (right-fork) path, following farm walls southeast and, just before High Rough, drop down onto Heights Road.

C   Turn right onto Heights Road and turn first left again, just before the Orange mast, down the surfaced track to Wadsworth Banks. You will have a clear view over Foster Clough in the nearground and Scout Wood beyond. Follow this road down past a goat farm, and bear right at the bottom onto Raw Lane. This lane also offers you superb views over to Cragg Vale, Erringden Moor and Rake Head. But stop at Winter Royd farmhouse on your left; look for its name in wrought-iron letters moulded into the gate, as it's an important marker.

D   A few metres before Winter Royd, follow the PF signpost to

28

the left of an iron gate and down the hill into a small but tranquilly beautiful wood. This wood is awash with bluebells in late spring and is always a very beautiful oasis. Zigzag down for about three hundred yards until the path smooths out and, at a gate and stile, meets the path at the eastern end of Burlees Lane. Turn left into the fields, over a stile and head southeast down the hill.

At this stage, the terrain may become a little difficult and the path hard to follow. Don't be tempted to head straight down into the clough, but follow the sheep-track around the hill (keeping its crest to your right) till it reaches a stone wall running north-south. Turn left here at an opening near the apex of wall and fence, and attack the clough this safer way.

E   You are now in Redacre Wood and Redacre Clough bickers down the hill to your left. This is a very pretty dell, the path taking you very steeply down to meet yet another mini-clough which burbles along from your right. Slosh through or nimbly vault the water, being very careful of tree-roots and mud as you reach the other side. A few more yards will take you to a tarmac road which tries to tempt you down via the new filter works to the canal and the A646. But instead, turn right uphill, through the farm buildings of Broadbottom, following the 'drive' until you meet a wooden gate and stile at a CW sign.

Bear right from here so that you follow the CW path along the bottom of Burlees Wood, a stone wall and fields to your left and the magnificent trees of the wood to your right. Emerge from the trees and saunter along a sort of ridge with the green fields of Long Royd to both your left and right.

F   You arrive at the tip of Fallingroyd Wood where a stile heralds the end of your present path. A few yards beyond, a deep, steep path heads down towards the canal. Join this path, then almost immediately cross over it to where it opens onto a south-facing field, just below Great Burlees. Cross down through the cow-field, heading for the western end of a long wall behind a row of houses. Then another north-south wall takes you into a second field with Higher May Royd Wood now to your left, high above and parallel to the A646.

From a rusted gate in the fence on your left, make your way down the path through the wood as if you were heading to the road. Once at a clearing and out of the trees, the path will take you upwards again over a couple more stiles and another mini-clough; soon you will see the houses of Dodd Naze up on your right (not that you are heading there). Leap over the water of the clough, and then a last stile will see you into Common Bank Wood above Machpelah. Bearing right across the wood, the path will bring you out, after a couple of hundred very pretty metres, onto Osborne Street at the bottom of Marlborough Road.

You are out of the woods! Now skip back down to Stubbings School, and remember that your just deserts may await you at the White Lion or at one of the coffee shops near St George's Square at the bottom of the hill. But I guess you'll be feeling so fresh after this little amble that you'll hardly need any extra refreshment. Or do I misjudge your capacities?

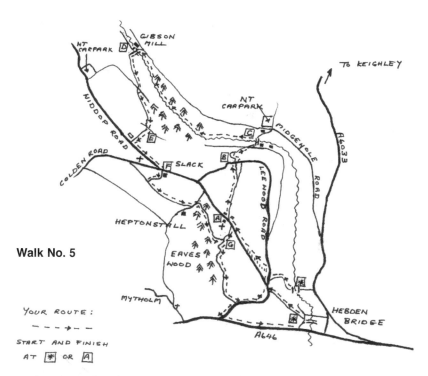

Walk No. 5

YOUR ROUTE:

– – – →– –

START AND FINISH

AT ✳ OR A

WALK NO. 5

WHERE CRAGS AND ROCKS CANNOT CORRUPT

*Heptonstall (GR986281) - Midgehole - Gibson Mill - Slack Top
- Hell Hole Rocks - Hebden Bridge*

Distance: 4.75 miles (7.5 km). Leave 3-4 hours
Conditions: Generally good; one steep descent and ascent
Level: Easy - medium

If you remember from the Introduction to this section, these walks are intended to keep local people on their feet and the car in the garage. So if you live in the Hebden Bridge valley or environs, please attempt to make your way to Heptonstall on foot; as a last resort, take the bus up. You'll feel a better person for it. The straightest and shortest route from Hebden Bridge (which a bus can't manage) is the Buttress, and there is also the less marginally less strenuous and equally un-bus-able Slater Bank path leading up from the river-end of Foster Lane. Both paths will lead you to the Lee Wood Road steps, the safer and pleasanter route up the Heptonstall Road.

This walk, like many others, is nicer on a dry day, but particularly because the stretch of path down to Hardcastle Crags is pretty slippery and steep, so bring your stick with you this time to help with your stability and leverage.

But what a delicious walk this is, taking you into our local pride and joy, Hardcastle Crags, and up through smooth fields to capture spellbinding views of our valley from the Widdop Road. If you should ever feel jaded with life in our valley, just get up here for a minute or so and you'll feel positively proud, possessive and pepped up - all over again.

A   At Weavers' Square, Heptonstall, and with the church behind you, cross over into Townfield Lane. You will pass Whitehall Fold on your right and a row of bungalows on your left, after which the lane becomes a farm track with stone wall on either side of you. Proceed through until you reach a gate, go through the gap and bear left across the fields until you reach the top stretch of Lee Wood Road. Already views over to Shackleton and Pecket Well are tantalising, but look ahead and take care as you cross the rather busy Draper Lane as it has blind bends. Once across, head left to a PF sign and a stile in the wall.

B **Once over the wall, head for the fence and stile with CW arrows,** and begin your lengthy descent down to Midgehole. The path steers you down left and is composed to start with of generous stone steps, but it soon becomes muddy and tortuous. Further down, it opens out into leafy glades and brings you to a tarmac single-track road: this is the road to Hebden Hey and care should be taken crossing it. Then bear right on the continuation of your path past Cairnacre Farmhouse on your right; you will emerge at the stone bridge at Midgehole.

C **Just over the bridge, turn left through the stone wall onto the river path to Gibson Mill.** Take your time; if you've never done this path, you'll want to savour the sounds of the water, the sights of the herons and the rock pools and weirs and lofty trees; if you're an old hand, you'll want to enjoy the exercise of the up-and-down rocks and tree-root staircases: great for the lissom body! Hebden Water throbs a rhythm to the pulse of your feet and you can feel quite high on it all. Follow the post-markers so that you find yourself safely, in a little under half an hour, at the elegant Gibson Mill, the mill which may look abandoned but which refuses to lie down and die and which is often in use as a meeting-place and promises to come back to life as an ecology centre.

D **At Gibson Mill, cross the stone bridge and turn immediately left, onto a track leading you up the hill away from the river.** After 250 metres or so (just after a wooden shelter on your right), the track will try to pull you around to the right and up to an NT carpark on Widdop Road; resist its pull and bear left onto a woodland path. Immediately you are on this ferny path (very hard to discern and literally a matter of three or four yards from its beginning), look for a path up to your right, shrouded in the greenery. (If the path you are on seems to be remaining straight and flat, then you have missed your turn; turn and retrace your steps to the 'junction' and start again; you should be travelling upwards almost straight away.) Mostly consisting of deep stone steps, this hill path becomes quite steep and slippery with moss in most weathers because the sun seldom penetrates this wooded, north-facing hillside, so do climb carefully. Savour it too: it's a private sort of route, a 'secret' path seldom used by run-of-the-mill visitors. Stop at the top of the path, should you need to get your breath back, at a gap in a stone wall which will lead you up into a field.

E   **Walk up through the field in front of you**, respectfully wide-berthing any livestock, but heading in a more or less straight line to the left of a Widdop Road farmhouse. This farm has recently installed a new stile onto the lower drive. Climb over it, then walk up the few metres to Widdop Road. Although you are now on tarmac and you need to take the usual care with traffic, regard this temporary 'aberration' as a wonderful opportunity to take in the gaspingly fabulous length and breadth of the Crags' valley: Widdop and Gorple behind you, Pecket Well and Mount Skip before you and Shackleton alongside you as you walk close to the road wall into Slack.

F   **Arriving at the fork in the Widdop/Colden Road at Slack Top, and with the Zionist chapel on your right,** cross the road so that you are on the south side of the junction and approach a (former B & B) farmhouse called Poppyfields House which has a PF sign beside it. Yes, you may enter: take the very private-looking footpath to the right of the house (no, you're not trespassing), go through a gap in the wall and out onto a grassy path behind a row of houses and gardens. Follow the fence around an unkempt field until a gravelled track crosses your path; turn left onto this. The views from here through Lumb Bank to Stoodley Pike are predictably stunning. Stay on the higher path and you will hit the tarmac again: the 'road' down to Lumb Bank. Turn left here and walk up this road for about 150 metres, until a CW post on your right will lead you off, through the wall roadside, onto a path delightfully leading you through the backstage area of Heptonstall: the woods and rocks of upper Eaves Wood. You plunge quite deep into the trees and start quite soon to clamber over rocks, so keep a close eye out for a 'turning' left taking you south and upwards all the time: you stay on the 'cliff top', a wonderful path over rocks and roots which requires a slightly slower pace. You have the boundary wall of the village to your left as you make your way to and above Hell Hole Rocks. The tower of the church soon comes into view as you make your way over the heart-stopping rock balconies. As the path opens out even more, equally heart-stopping views over to Stoodley and down the valley to Charlestown and Eastwood stop you in your tracks. All this beauty so close to home! It is an exhilarating route back into the village.

G   The path which has you suspended over Hell Hole Rocks, and which continues down to further dramatic rock walls, gives you a choice: return to Heptonstall village by taking the walled path to the left, over Beckett Drive and into West Laithe, back to the centre of the village, emerging either at Weavers' Square or Cloth Hall and facing the choice of the Cross or the White Lion; or pick your way down through the grass to pick up the extension of your path, which then zigzags you down, past amazing rock walls where climbers may no doubt be exercising their masochism, and down over the beautiful wooded then rocky path - with views of Mytholm and Hebden Bridge all the way - down to lower Heptonstall Road where you may drop down, either left to pick up the Buttress once more, or right to pick up the stone steps down to the Co-Op and the A646.

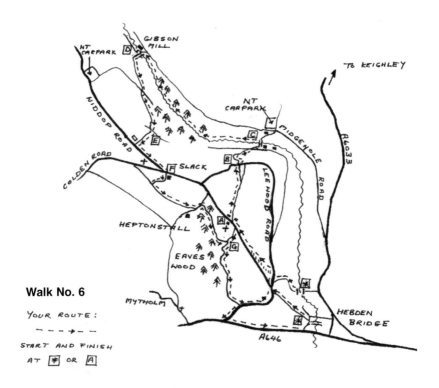

Walk No. 6

YOUR ROUTE:

− − − →− − −

START AND FINISH

AT ✱ OR A

WALK NO. 6

DELF END DELIGHTS

The Nutclough (GR995276) - Old Town - Delf End
- Pecket Well - Midgehole - Hebden Bridge

Distance: 4.75 miles (7.5 km). Leave 3 hours
Conditions: Most often, muddy and wet in places; an initial steep
                 ascent. Good ridge paths
Level: Medium

Take a balmy spring evening, heady with scents of burgeoning elder
and cow-parsley, and climb through them until you reach the sky -
where the blues and greens of your valley are left behind for the
golden glow of twilight - and you will feel truly in heaven.

This is a wonderful walk for after work when you can wash away
the day's grime with the goodness of the air and the whispering of the
trees, and when you feel as refreshed as if you'd just bathed in a
limpid pool: perfect mental and physical restoratives available in the
hills above our valley. So do yourselves and the dog a favour: pull on
your shorts and boots and get out there.

Starting and finishing once again at the Nutclough Woods, this
walk is generally gentle, despite some steep ascents to begin with. But
once up on the ridges, you stride along their broad backs with ease
and sweep high around their pleasing curves.

Have a pair of binoculars in your rucksack this time, in case the
spring birds try to enchant you without identifying themselves.

**A   Starting at the Keighley Road entrance to the Nutclough
Woods, go north up the hill**, taking the left-hand path of the clough,
up the old mill steps past the pond and high into the lofty woods. Just
beyond the handsome stone bridge and just before the now-defunct
pump house, peel off left onto a thin, heather-lined path up the steep
hill to your left. Take a breather when you reach the first wall, because
the climb has been a stiff little one and because the views over
Hebden Bridge from this point are restorative in themselves and offer

a foretaste of the beauty of the rest of the walk. Then carry on over the hill above you and step over a stile into a walled pathway taking you to Club Houses and Walker Lane.

B   Turn left and follow Walker Lane upwards until you reach its junction with Billy Lane. Cross straight over the road, taking the walled path between a field on your left and houses on your right. Ascend the hill and, at a junction with a farm track, bear right; as you climb, you will find Wall Stones Reservoir on your left, and that you are heading towards Bog Eggs Farmhouse. Walk courteously through the farm to a wall at the northern end of the 'garden'. (Conversely, you can skirt the farm to its left, making your way first through heather and then through sheep fields to meet the same north wall.) At this point you are almost in the 'wilds', out of the confines of clipped, cultivated land and into the fabulous freedom of the moors.

C   The Bog Eggs Edge wall (try saying that correctly at the end of the walk) borders a broad stretch of the CW Way. Now turn left and, ignoring the path which tries to lure you up to the right towards High Brow Knoll (a later walk in this series), follow the path which now leads you northwest towards Pecket Well. With the wall on your left, it will lead you past Moorside Farmhouse - the slopes to High Brown Knoll pulling away to your right - until you reach an iron gate which will land you up on an unsurfaced track which forms a 'junction' with Delf End. Turn left (south) down this track (Slack House Lane) as if you were making directly for Pecket Well, but about 150 metres down where the track steers left, go right (northwest) to follow the stone wall around Aberdeen Flat. It is a little swampy around here, but let the rushes and sludginess be your assurance that you are on the correct route. Start watching for a gap in the wall where you will begin to make your descent to Pecket Well.

D   You have found the right field if there is a small reservoir in it. The field may appear too swampy to cross easily, but grip the left-hand wall and you can make your way quite drily to the other side. On the south side of the field, you will find another opening through a wall; step through it and onto a wide farm track, taking you down past Hill Top Farmhouse to Wilcroft Terrace and the Keighley Road.

E **Turn right onto the Keighley Road and walk very carefully (for there is no proper footpath on either side of this stretch of the road) up to the bus-turning at Crimsworth Lane.** (Don't think of hailing a bus. You're not through with beauty yet!) Turn left down this lane past a collection of farmhouses until, at the hub of this little settlement, you will find a signpost to Pecket Well monument, taking you down via a pleasant hillside path out onto open fields and into the enclosure where the monument stands: a mini-version of Stoodley Pike but this time commemorating local war-fallen. Spend some inspiring minutes here, your contemplation enhanced by the humbling beauty of the views over our valley. Doesn't it all make you feel just so lucky to be here?

F **Once you've taken your fill, leave the enclosure by going left down the path towards Pecket Well Clough,** where throbbing water tumbles down at Kitling Bridge and where the leafy overhang creates a magical beauty-spot. Cross the bridge and turn right onto the downhill path to Midgehole, behind the Dying and Finishing Works, and emerge at a cluster of mill and farm buildings onto the tarmac of Midgehole Road.

G **Turn left onto the road and walk about 200 metres until you reach Raw Holme house;** bear right here onto the usually muddy path which then takes you, down steep steps on your right, over Lee Mill Road and onto the river path. Cross the bridge at the Bowling Club and you will reach the Archery Club at Slater Bank bridge (the west end of Foster Lane). Hasten your step now, either along Foster Lane to the Keighley Road, or around Victoria Road to Valley Road, as you seek a self-congratulatory refreshment in a Hebden Bridge pub.

Ready for sleep and refreshed for the next day's work, I reckon you'll agree that this walk beats a night in with the telly - any day!

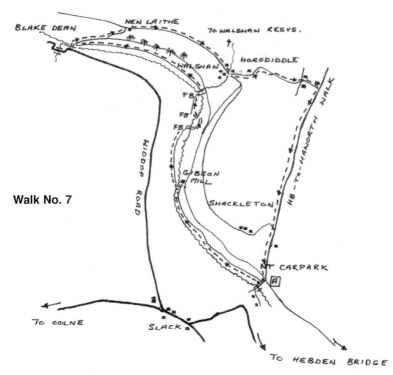

Walk No. 7

WALK NO. 7

BLAKE DEAN BECKONING

Midgehole (GR989292) - Gibson Mill - Blake Dean
- Horodiddle - Midgehole - **Hebden Bridge**

Distance: 6.75 miles (11 km). Leave 4-5 hours
Conditions: Generally firm and good; some wet and slippery
                 sections near Blake Dean
Level: Medium

If you take this walk in the summer, you can be extra-specially
rewarded with a bathe in the balmy waters of Blake Dean, so have
your swimming kit with you just in case. Or if you walk this one in
June, you may also be lucky and find yourself followed on your route
by the haunting company of the sculptures in the annual Hardcastle
Crags Sculpture Trail, so clever timing of this walk should make the
very most of it.

    It certainly is a summery walk: offering sun and shade, forest, field
and fell, livestock galore and plant-life aplenty - once again a walk of
infinite variety. When I last did this walk on a damp spring day,
cuckoo-song followed me up the river; an owl sedately swooped
across it; a heron stood motionless by its banks; clumps of primroses
lapped at the water and the 'rhodos' were rampant. The lambs were
fussing in the fields and the calves eyed me seductively. All this can
be yours too; get out there while it's gorgeous.

A   **At Midgehole, from the road facing the National Trust
carpark, turn left down the lane towards the river.** Just past the stone
cottage and before the bridge, go right through a gap in the wall and
down onto the river-path which leads you happily to Gibson Mill. At
a stroll, this stretch usually takes about half an hour, but savour your
surroundings: enjoy clambering over the boulders as the path takes
you close to the river and winding up into the glades as it takes you
away from it.

B   **At Gibson Mill, go through the mill-yard and over the**

bridge. Turn right and follow the path past two placid mill-ponds (one on your right and the other, a little further on where you strut the parapet between river and mill-pond, on your left). The path then becomes rockier and wetter, so start watching your step for a bit, until it evens out with the help of flag-stones and even the occasional stretch of wooden decking. The path will lead you, for about half a mile, over three wooden footbridges: at the third footbridge, where the river-route seemingly comes to an end, turn sharp left (ignoring the rough tracks leading up the hill). Though it becomes less easy to follow at this point, keep on the narrow path, with the river on your left. For a while, this is really quite difficult underfoot: over stones and mini-brooks and slippery moss, but do persist because it soon becomes safer ground and, within a quarter of a mile or so, the path widens and the shrouding cover of trees lifts its curtain on a new scene: the broad valley of Blake Dean.

C   You may not believe the change: you suddenly find yourself in the most dramatic setting. You might realistically think you were somewhere else entirely: a Scottish glen for example. It's not all easy walking at this stage because you have to weave your way around rocks and through the clumsily tossed rubble from the old bridge pylons. (You may already know that these are what remains of the five base-pillars of the wooden bridge which used to straddle this valley when, in 1900, a steam railway transported materials for the construction of the Walshaw Dean reservoirs.) It is a strangely quiet and even eerie landscape, especially when you ponder the touching memorial on one of the rocks to "Felix and Rupert" and their father, whose lives tragically ended in this valley. It slows you down, this place, as if there's an opiate in the air. Walk as far as the footbridge and pick a grassy spot: for a picnic, a dip in the crisp waters, or just some moments of quiet reflection.

D   When you feel you've had your fill, start to make your way out of the Dean. Remaining on the same side of the valley as you entered it and with your back to the footbridge, take the path up the hill to your right. When you reach the crest, turn left at a fork in the path before it tries to take you straight ahead and plunge you back into the woods of the Crags; you are now going to stay in open country for a while. Your path will now lead you up the hill through a sheep-field to a gate on the road at New Laithes. Turn right here and walk along this road (which eventually leads to Shackleton) through the very pretty group of houses (ta very much, tug the forelock to m'Lord Savile in his shooting seat - if it weren't for him, we wouldn't have the Crags at all). Ignoring the signposted track leading off sharp left, continue east past the houses and, about 50 yards further on, fork left off the road: go up a slight rise and through a farm gate where you are signposted to Crimsworth Dean. The route will now take you through the fields of Horodiddle, past a farmhouse on your left and through another gate at a dip. Then, keeping the stone wall close on your left, follow the path around to your right and up the hill. At a wooden signpost, go through the gate in the wall and continue your path east, but with the wall now on your right.

After a few hundred yards, the path will take you sharply downhill at an old stone gateway and two ruined farm buildings, one each on either side of you, guiding you down the track (now walled on both sides) to a T-junction: this is the main Haworth-to-Hebden Bridge path - leading left to Lumb Falls and the Old Haworth Road, and right to Midgehole and Hebden Bridge.

E   Turn right and make your way down, for almost a mile, to your starting point at the NT carpark. On your way down, you will pass the Shackleton turn-off on your right and the NT office on your left - before you arrive once again at Midgehole.

You may take either a bus back to Hebden Bridge (advance knowledge of the timetable is important) or just a gentle walk back to town via the Bowling Club and the Archery Club (see Walk no. 6). Sadly, you have not passed a hostelry on your way, but the trusty White Lion is your nearest and is very walker-sympathetic. Why not just head smartly to it, allowing your energies to flag only when you have your feet up and your hands around a pint of the best?

Walk No. 8

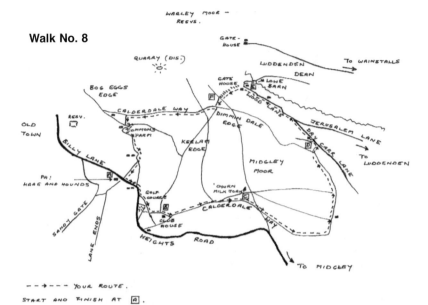

-- →---- YOUR ROUTE.
START AND FINISH AT A .

WALK NO. 8:

RING AROUND THE MOORS

*Old Town (Billy Lane) (GR004280) - Midgley Moor
- Castle Carr - Dimmin Dale - Bog Eggs Edge - Old Town*

Distance: 6.5 miles (10 km). Leave 3-4 hours
Conditions: Generally good to excellent. One very steep ascent
Level: Medium

This walk is something of a magic circle: an enchanting ring around Midgley Moor, taking in entrancing views and beauty-spots. The landscape changes almost imperceptibly so that, as you step out of one terrain and into another, you'll be left wondering whether the last one was real or not. Magic, see?

You might want to have your camera with you, as the valleys and their flora will hold beauties you may not be able to describe - and perhaps a pair of binoculars in your rucksack to make the most of fabulous views and interesting wildlife. As usual, sturdy boots are a must because of the different conditions you will meet, and, if it's a warm day, have a flask of water aboard. Remember that one quite steep ascent awaits you; it is within the capabilities of most accustomed walkers, but be wise and take it slowly. Be reassured, however: it's basically Calderdale Way most of the way and that makes for very pleasant and well-maintained paths.

A At the Hare and Hounds pub, set yourself on Billy Lane and walk east up the road for about three hundred yards, around the bend past Little and Middle Nooks until, at the speed-derestriction sign, you bear right off the road onto a rough track towards the Hebden Bridge Golf Club. This little 'link' path will take you past a small quarry on your right, then to a stile at a 'Caution' sign: step onto the fairway of the golf course and, taking extreme care of flying balls and respecting the priority of golfers, head directly uphill to the left of the clubhouse, to meet another stile at the northern boundary fence of the course. Once out of harm's way, turn right, walking past and above the clubhouse, eastwards onto the Calderdale Way.

B **Following the clearly marked path for about 200 yards, climb over a stile (between gate and signpost) onto open heather-clad moor.** There is a comfortable flag-stoned stretch of path to help you through the bogland until, after another 200 yards, you reach a two-way signpost at a wall; keep this fine stone wall on your right for about 300 metres, then bear right, down through grassy tussocks (bypassing the path up to Churn Milk Joan, the imposing six-foot borderstone which stands, like a waiting golf-widow, at the crest of the hill to your left). The wall will take you round a 'corner' to the right so that you now face Scout Rocks beyond the river and you get fine views over to Cragg Vale and Erringden Moor.

C **Now bear left away from the wall, first heading slightly downhill towards Midgley, then up the hill again at the second of two close-set CW posts.** For a good while, you will have the comfort of a soft grassy path and of regular Calderdale Way posts to guide your traverse around Midgley Moor. Soak up the views and play 'dodgems' with the sheep, safe in the knowledge that your path is well-defined. After about 250 metres, you will meet a new wall on your right, the path now taking you gently eastwards towards Luddenden; head towards the next obvious farmhouse to your right. Keep on the Calderdale Way until you can see across to Wainstalls and the wind farm on Ovenden Moor. Then watch for a second farmhouse a little lower down on your right (Green House Farm), and continue for about 300 metres. Ignoring the first stile in the wall, continue to a second stile beside a metal gate and come off the Calderdale Way, crossing into the lane on the other side of it. Turn left onto a concrete farm track, then turn right until this track meets Dry Carr Lane.

D **Turn left into Dry Carr Lane. You are travelling northwest above beautiful Luddenden Dean. Ignoring the first little road on your left** with its 'No Through Road' sign, continue to the bottom of the road (just before it bends sharply right towards Jerusalem Farm) and turn left into Wood Lane. This little lane is utterly photogenic: below you is the handsome house of Upper Mytholm and the startling prettiness of Luddenden Brook. The lane itself is lined with dog-rose and wild fox-glove; it dips and twists and gives spellbinding views across to Saltonstall. It will take you past Catherine House

Farm, then even deeper into the valley where you will hear the river babbling away to your right - as far as the twin towers of the gate-house of Castle Carr. This surprising eccentricity is now transformed into two handsome houses, but it once formed part of the eighteenth -century building project of one Captain Joseph Priestley Edwards - who died in a railway accident before his grand dream mansion and gardens were ever completed. Later owners simply found the estate too expensive to maintain and the main house was demolished in the 1960s.

E **Stroll under the archway of the gatehouse at Low Lodge. Take the road around to the right to the bridge over Luddenden Brook at Lowe Barn** and take in the view up to the second of the two gatehouses on the Castle Carr Road from Wainstalls. Then return to Low Lodge where a rusted set of gates stands on your right. Straight ahead of you is a signpost to Old Town (via Keelam Gate); go through the slatted gate here and up the grassy path - which soon becomes stone-stepped, then timber-stepped to help ease your journey up. Be warned: it becomes very steep indeed and is quite long, so take your time and perhaps stop occasionally for breath and views. There is one thoughtful stage where the path flattens out for a minute or two to take you through bracken, but then it strikes up and steepens again - until at the top you clamber thankfully over the tumbled-down rocks of a wall and onto a track. Respire deeply and pat yourself on the sweaty back.

F **Cross straight over the track (ignoring the choices of going left or right), taking a fainter path through grass back onto the moor.** Soon your path joins a broader one which comes round to meet you on your left; bear right onto it. You are now on Dimmin Dale Edge. On the horizon to the west, you will see a disused quarry head; from this point bear left - southwesterly now - over the hill towards Old Town (you are not going right towards Keelam Edge), over into the valleys of home - with Stoodley Pike to greet you and even faraway Widdop calling out for your attention.

As you make your way over the hill, the path will take you towards a solitary farmhouse near Bog Eggs Edge. Just before you reach it, strike out left at a tiny path through the heather towards another farm-house. This one is readily identifiable because in its garden stands the straw-bail bathhouse constructed some years ago now by the amazing Amazon Nails team. Follow the fence to your right, and when you reach a metal gate and stile, cross into the short track to the farmhouse, then turn sharp left onto the road in front of it.

You are now in the last arc of your magic circle. Walk down this very stony track for about half a mile - until it becomes Popples Lane which joins Billy Lane, and the Hare and Hounds stands beckoning in front of you. The very hospitable landlords will be happy to pour you a pint of their best - so let's hope you've hit opening hours.

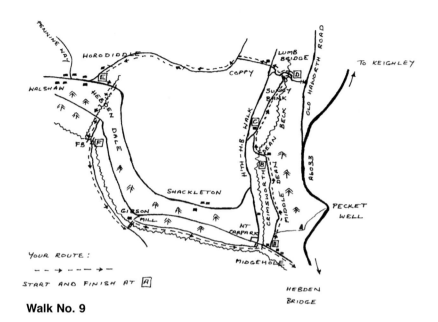

Walk No. 9

49

WALK NO. 9

GOING GREEN

*Midgehole (GR990291) - Crimsworth Dean - Lumb Falls - Horodiddle - Walshaw - Hardcastle Crags - Midgehole - **Hebden Bridge***

Distance:	6.5 miles (10 km). Leave 4-5 hours, to include time at Lumb Falls
Conditions:	Mostly soft but often damp underfoot; one or two steep ascents
Level:	Easy - medium

Go green! Take a totally eco-friendly walk which will immerse you in nothing but green: either wading through fields of shoulder-high bracken or winding through the deep, dark woods of Crimsworth Dean, you bathe yourself in a sea of cool green - until you emerge onto the wide hills of Horodiddle - where you feel you might be walking on the sky's beach. This is a wonderfully refreshing walk for a hot August day. Who needs the seaside when the environs of Hebden Bridge have all the elements?

A   At Midgehole, take the stony path up to the right of the public conveniences, veering left after about 75 yards onto a path signposted to the Haworth Old Road. Go through a rusted iron gate onto the old coach-road with its stone walls on both sides. This path opens out onto a grassy field and, as you head up the hill, a fine old mill wall offers to guide you into gorgeous Middle Dean Wood. After a squeeze through a narrow gap between the wall and a fence, follow the path around to the right and up into the hemline of the wood. Then bear left and into the thick of the trees. You are entering a dramatic river valley: on your left, the rock walls of the river deepen at every step, the water starts to thunder and you and the wall stand humbled above it. The path shrouds you in shadows and little sunlight penetrates. Go through a rather austere-looking iron gateway which may have once formed part of the mill boundary and you will now be led off the mill wall onto terra firma: with the filtering light of day now guiding you out of the wood. Bear right, taking a bit of a steep climb towards an opening in the stone wall ahead of you.

B   Go through the slatted gate in the wall and out into a marshy field, now affording bright daylight - we hope - and views over to Shackleton Knoll. Continue through into the next field where you cross a tiny spring at some rocks; your path then opens out again to lead you towards a farmhouse. (A third field awaits you first, with a set of stepping-stones to help you through its sogginess.) You reach what looks like a private gate into the farmhouse garden but, unless you are a cyclist, you are invited through: this is Lower Small Shaw. Just before the entrance to the handsome farmhouse, turn left and follow the fence down the hill to cross the stone bridge across Crimsworth Dean Beck. Then bear right and uphill, away from the beck and through a very pleasant stand of pines; a stile will take you into the open valley of Crimsworth Dean. The path here is quite steep but it will soon lead you onto a farm track at Charles Rough.

C   Turn right onto the farm track and make as if directly to the farmhouse ahead of you - peeling off right just before it onto a path which takes you behind the farm: a boggy path to begin with, but a 'musical' one, as you can hear the water of Crimsworth Dean singing away to your right. Go over a high stone wall with the help of its side-steps and into a field of exclusively bracken. In summer, the path here is green and soft underfoot and the bracken so deep that you can see only the sky overhead: it is appropriately named Sunny Bank, leading you towards the valley floor at Lumb Falls. At an ancient stone gatepost, veer right down the last section of the path.

And aren't the Falls beautiful? On a sunny, hot day, you might decide to linger: to picnic on the banks or to bathe in the safer waters to the north of the gate. This spot is a favourite with hardy boys who like to hazard all and plunge into the pools, but they can be deceptively shallow and their rocks are very slippery. Small children and dogs should be kept under the closest supervision. But with the beauty of the place almost incomparable, I guess you won't want to just rush away.

D   Turn back on yourself and walk out of the Falls the way you came in - now going southwest up to the stone gatepost - then bear right and straight up the hill. The path is rocky and a testing little climb, but views to your left over to Stoodley Pike should compensate for your efforts. Just past a couple of dilapidated barns and ignoring the bend in the path to your left, continue straight up; it's a steep ascent but you will soon emerge onto the Haworth-to-Hebden Bridge Walk route, a broad farm track. Go through the gate on your right and turn immediately left off the main track. You are now heading, uphill again, towards Horodiddle and Walshaw via Coppy. Once through another gate at the top, veer left, the path now turning southwest and introducing you to a range of glorious views: first to Walshaw and Widdop, then to the glinting Gorple Reservoirs, and beyond to the hills of Lancashire - while at your feet, heather is pink on the moors beside you and curlews dart, quorkling in alarm, from the low bushes.

About 300 metres along this path, a wooden signpost steers you through a gate in the wall into a sheep field. Stick close to the wall (now on your right) and make your way down this glorious open hillside towards Walshaw. Go through a gate, then across a culverted stream and over a small rise onto the Shackleton-Walshaw road.

E   At the hamlet of Walshaw, turn left onto the firm gravel road, and saunter down to the bridge about 200 metres away. Squeeze through the tiny gap in the bridge wall on your right, and drop down into what I call the 'rhododendron jungle' of Hebden Dale: this is a beautiful clough, a chillingly cool spot even on the hottest day and always pretty squidgy underfoot. And you may have to duck your head as you go to avoid being garrotted by the rhodos! In spring, it's the gorgeous colours of the shrubs that dazzle; in summer, it's their density that astonishes. The increasingly muddy path will take you over three tiny footbridges; do not cross the fourth bridge but stay on the right of the water, to be led firstly up the breast of a hill, then steeply down until you reach the stone wall which borders the Hardcastle Crags road. Go through a gap in the wall, then over a metal culvert, turn immediately right and stroll through a wide clearing down to Hebden Water.

F   At Hebden Water, cross the fine wooden footbridge and turn left (putting you on the right of the water) and begin to make your way down to Gibson Mill: the familiar and comforting amble over footbridges and stone shelves, to follow the river through leafy glades into the quieter waters of the mill. This is Sculpture Trail territory and probably well known to most of you. From Gibson Mill, take another half-hour or so to return to the NT carpark at Midgehole, either by road or, preferably, by the captivating river path (see Walk no. 7, part A, in reverse).

You could bus it back to town from Midgehole (if you know the timetable in advance and aren't kept waiting in inclement weather for too long), but why not walk in via the now-familiar Bowling and Archery Clubs route, and stop for some refreshment at one of our 'greener' cafés on Market Street, Hebden Bridge.

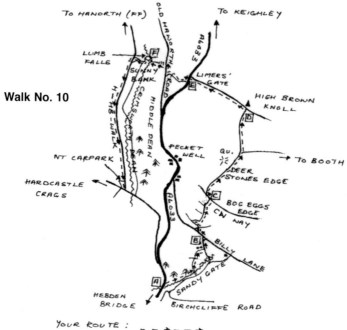

Walk No. 10

WALK NO. 10

HIGH BROWN ROUTE TO TAKE YOU
AWAY FROM IT ALL

Nutclough Woods (GR995276) - Old Town - High Brown Knoll - Lumb Falls - Crimsworth Dean - Midgehole - Hebden Bridge

Distance:	6.5 miles (10 km). Leave 3-4 hours, to include time at Lumb Falls
Conditions:	Generally good. Boggy towards Summer Rake Edge, and one or two steep descents and ascents
Level:	Medium

Ever feel like climbing up the nearest hill and screaming your lungs out? Or finding yourself somewhere where you are completely on your own, can see no civilisation for miles and feel right away from it all? Then let this walk take you there - and remember to bring along your binoculars.

At its height, this walk will afford you three hundred and sixty-degree views of - nowhere in particular. Nothing to speak of - but air and birdsong and staggering light and acres of green, brown and blue. From where it is taking you - high, high up on the moors - you can't see Halifax or Huddersfield, you can't see Bingley or Bradford or even Mytholmroyd and Hebden Bridge. The most built-up landmark is Heptonstall and that's no urban threat to your claustrophobia or peace of mind.

With none of these towns more than 15 miles away, it's something of a miracle that they are invisible; but the hills and valleys hug each other so close that their settlements are simply hidden, while you feel your chest-cage expand at the openness of it all and you can do what we so often forget to do: breathe!

A **From the Nutclough Woods entrance on the Keighley Road, walk north up into the steep woodlands, climbing up its left-hand path** and following the trees and the sound of gushing water, as far as the stone bridge. Then, just opposite the old pumping house, peel off up to the left, taking the tiny track through the heather and winding you up very steeply to a stone wall. Stop here at the stile, catch your breath and take in the already wonderful view over Hebden Bridge and the Calder Valley to the south. Press on through the next field, over the hill, until you see the Mitchell Bros. mill chimney at Old Town come into view. A second stone wall will take you into a pretty walled path that leads up to the terrace known as Club Houses.

B   Turn left onto Walker Lane and walk up to the junction with Billy Lane. Turn left here and follow the road-wall for about 75 yards until it gives you a right turn into another walled path (handsome horses will no doubt be in the fields to either side of you). Walk up the track, cross over an east-west-running path and then on to a steeper, grassier slope. At the top, turn left onto the main track (which leads around Wall Stones Hill and through its quarries) and follow it for about 100 yards until it clearly takes a sharp right. Continue your path up and over the hill - straight ahead on a stony track, then along a tiny path through a field of heather.

Head towards the right-hand corner of a stone wall. Bog Eggs Edge lies straight ahead of you and you can already see the 'cutting' into its western end that you will soon be taking; Bog Eggs farmhouse stands on your right. Go through the wall-opening and through another two fields, following their right-hand walls. At the top, cross the stile in the wall facing you onto the Calderdale Way at Bog Eggs Edge.

C   Turn left onto the Calderdale Way and, almost immediately, bear right up the hill onto a grassy 'cutting': clearly an old transport track to and from the now-disused quarries which you will soon see over the hill. Follow its broad, clear track up the hill, past the wonderfully evocative quarry at Delf End Flat, the old boundary walls of which the sheep now use as their home, running in and out of the 'doors' as you approach as if to express ownership.

The path opens out broadly at Deer Stones Edge. Look left and take in the famous traditional views to Widdop and Gorple, Haworth Moor and Horodiddle - and feel your pulse start to quicken. As you reach the ridge, the path will now bear you either right towards Luddenden and Booth, or left - via Summer Rake Edge - up to the Knoll; follow the left-hand path. It will get progressively boggier as it takes you over the routes well used by fell runners and mountain bikes, so you'll be pleased you are wearing sturdy boots.

D **After your exhilarating climb, stop at the stumpy white trig-point at High Brown Knoll and get out your binoculars.** You'll be amazed as much at what you can't see as what you can. Look out for yachts on Warley Moor Reservoir and the wind generators on Ovenden Moor. Move around for 360 degrees and marvel at the sameness of it all: hills and moors and sky. It's likely you'll be approached by the odd chatty bike-rider or walker who'll stop and share your gasps of wonder, or it might be that your only companion is the squawking of the grouse and the croaking of the curlews - or you may hear nothing at all. It is truly wonderful and will give you a tremendous sense of reward for all your hard walk.

When you have drunk your fill, turn to the north and follow the path left (northwest) across Limers' Gate and Naze End where the old stones tell their tales of resting wayfarers and loaded ponies labouring between Lancashire and Yorkshire. This inspiring path takes you over the brow of Naze Hill and you find yourself on the short but summary descent down to the Keighley Road.

E **When you reach the wooden gate at the bottom onto the A6033, turn left onto the road, cross over it and walk down for about 75 metres (watching very carefully for speeding cars)** until you reach a gate on the right with its comforting yellow CW arrow. Cross into this field and take its boggy path down to a second gate where you are invited down a walled track onto the Old Haworth Road. Turn right onto the road and walk along it for about 100 metres until a path on your left signposts you down the stony and quite steep descent to Lumb Falls.

Because my last walk also took in Lumb Falls, you won't need reminding either of its beauties nor of its hazards. Take your time here and, when you are ready, cross the bridge, go through the rusted metal gate and make your way up out of the Falls by the western path.

F **Climb as far as the huge stone post and stop and make a decision: either a) to return to Midgehole by walking (the reverse of) the route I gave you in Walk no. 9 - via the leafy dells of Crimsworth Dean Beck and Middle Dean Wood** - but you should only take this path if you refer to Walk no. 9 to bone up on its complicated bits, or **b) to stay on the walled path up the hill to Sunny Bank,** until it meets the main track of the Haworth-to-Hebden Bridge Walk.

Assuming you take **b)**, turn left once at the top and troop down the farm track with its fabulous views back into the Upper Calder Valley and over to Stoodley Pike and which soon becomes the National Trust road (you will pass the NT farmhouse office at Hollins Hall) down to the carpark at Midgehole - where you might also meet your fellow-walkers who are emerging from the Middle Dean path.

Walk along Midgehole Road to the Keighley Road - or via our now familiar Bowling and Archery Club route - into Hebden Bridge and refresh yourself with more humanity than you have seen in a few hours and with more civilisation on tap than the lonely moors afforded you. With a pint of landlord's in your hand, it might be a tough choice as to which you would prefer.

Walk No. 11

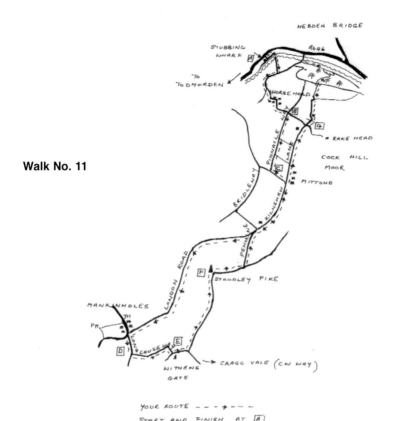

WALK NO. 11

THE BLACK INGOT BECKONS

*Stubbing Wharf (GR983272) - Horsehold - London Road
- Mankinholes - Stoodley Pike - Crow Wood - **Hebden Bridge***

Distance: 7.5 miles (12 km). Leave 4 hours
Conditions: Muddy and wet in parts, especially in winter, and
                  one steep ascent
Level: Medium

When the fogs and rains and muds of autumn return, there's only one attitude to take: if you can't beat 'em, join 'em. We can't expect to stay fit and well throughout the bleak seasons unless we meet them head on. Kitted out thoroughly, you can confidently tackle the wettest of walks: at the same time savour the russet colours, the peaty scents and the biting air of autumn and winter. So bring out the boots and check their tread; unwrap the cagoule and check its seams. And while you're rummaging, why not drag out the gaiters, telescopic walking stick and overtrousers - all items which, before I came to live in the Pennines from the antipodes, I used to dismiss as eccentric - how soon I was to learn!

What about an amble up to stout and Stoodley Pike? My only provisos would be, firstly, that, if you are unfamiliar with the pathways in that area, it is seriously unwise to venture up on a foggy day (and anyway, you'll want a clear day for the best views from the top); and secondly, be prepared for one steep ascent from Lumbutts up the Long Causeway. But otherwise this should be a steady, straight and pleasant walk in almost any weather.

A   **At Stubbing Wharf, turn left onto the canal towpath behind the pub, and cross the stone bridge that faces you.** A stepped path on your right will lead you past a house and straight up the hill, a fairly slippery climb for about 300 metres to bring you to the Horsehold Road. Turn right onto the road and walk up into the rather 'aromatic' farm hamlet of Horsehold. Once through the settlement, follow the road up the hill until, at a 'junction' with a field path and a farm track, you meet the Pinnacle Way. Already the open fields are offering enticing views across to your destination, and the visible challenges should be firing up your adrenaline.

B **Turn right onto the Pinnacle Way. You will pass Pinnacle Farm on your right,** the mud created by family cattle severely slowing your pace - but the track soon becomes firmer and grassier. In fact, a little way on, your path becomes plain glorious, openly revealing the terrain you will be conquering: the fine long ridge of Cock Hill Moor and its imposing spur from where the black ingot beckons you upwards. Your step will become lighter and sprightly whatever the conditions underfoot. Soon, after a rusted iron gate, the walled path takes you through two sheep fields, then a gate in the boundary wall will take you onto a clearly defined farm track.

C **Turn left, go through the iron gate and walk straight ahead (east); once through the iron gate at the top, turn right onto Kilnshaw Lane,** from where Stoodley Pike looks so close you can almost touch it. At Swillington Farm on your right, go through its rusted iron gate and in no time the Pennine Bridleway crosses your path. For now you are to stay on the historic London Road which, as you can see ahead of you, will take you round the western side of Stoodley Hill and Higher Moor.

London Road in this century is merely a rocky and muddy farm track. Go through the gate set into the wall ahead of you and enjoy the tramp around the hillside. Wonderful views, over the deep valley of Height Wood through to the hills of East Lancashire, lie before you. Look up to your left: see and sense the gloomy power of Stoodley Pike which hovers overhead and leads you around the hill. Soon the houses of Mankinholes will come into view, but you will no doubt be keeping an equal eye on your feet, as streams run off the hills and converge on this path so it is rarely dry - in winter, it's pretty horrible. After almost a mile of this track, a wooden gate will alert you to its imminent end and your arrival in Mankinholes.

D **You emerge onto the smooth, drained tarmac at Mankinholes. (Although your planned route will take you immediately left,** linger if you will: turn right and wander past the attractive houses and, opposite the particularly handsome Youth Hostel, turn left into a field whose flagged path will take you directly to the Top Brink pub, where a warm welcome and pint will await you - even on a Sunday when it's full to the brink with families and roast lamb.)

Back at the pathways where you emerged from Hebden Bridge, turn onto a broad track signposted as the Calderdale Way. Head steadily for the hill, pacing yourself for a stiff climb. Once through the next wooden gate, turn left as signposted: to Cragg Vale via Long Causeway. This is the centuries-old packhorse route which once saw daily traders, as well as coffin corteges, ply their way over the hills to Heptonstall. The flagged path may look long and straight, but soon enough it will veer left and take away some of the gradient for you. You will thankfully approach the ridge where four ways meet at a signpost: this is the wonderful Withens Gate, a historic crossroads which once carried construction transport and which is well worn down by the feet of your forebears and their horses. Nearby stands the fine stone called Long Stoop, an ancient marker post.

E   Turn left onto the Pennine Way and enjoy a rocky scramble over the hillocks (East Scout and High Stones), the 'hinterland' of Stoodley Pike, towards a 'plateau' where clambering over the casually tossed rocks is more reminiscent of exploring rock-pools at the seaside than tramping the moors. You will need to watch your step, as this rocky stretch to the Pike is deceptively long. But once on safe, smooth ground, you can start to absorb the inspiring views to the left of you.

At the Pike, you will want to stop: breathe, relax and recover, probably climb the historic Pike of the Turbulent Health Record and give it some moral support. It needs our respect: it is our permanent reference-point, a ubiquitous and reassuring landmark which no longer collapses on us - as it used to.

F   Leave the Pike by continuing down the Pennine Way in an easterly direction, crossing the famous spring at the Public Slaketrough (go on, try the water; it's vintage!), until you reach a boundary wall. Once over it, climb the stile in the wall on your left and make your way down the hill which gives you beautiful views over the grid of walled fields to Horsehold and Heptonstall. At the bottom, you will hit Kilnshaw Lane (the London Road) once again. Bear right onto the road, not turning left towards Pinnacle Way this time; instead, you pass Mittons farmhouses on your right and Erringden Grange on your left, to arrive at a junction: left to Horsehold and right up to Rake Head.

G   **Go straight over the junction, onto a rockier farm track which winds down the hill towards Hebden Bridge:** first to the left; then, just where it steers right, take the grassy path which leads straight down the hill. The path becomes walled on both sides and cuts into the hill, to take you under the Old Chamber road and out into Crow Wood. Once through the wood, either path will lead you down onto Palace House Road. A left turn will soon have you back at the canal towpath and installed at Stubbing Wharf pub with its beguiling variety of guest beers and a warm welcome to even the muddiest of walkers.

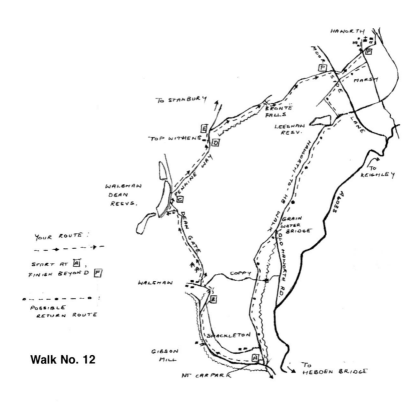

Walk No. 12

WALK NO. 12

HAWORTH HISTORY, LITERATURE
AND LANDSCAPE

*Midgehole (GR989292) - Gibson Mill
- Walshaw - Top Withens - **Haworth***

Distance: 8.75 miles (14 km). Leave 4 hours one way
Conditions: Generally excellent
Level: Medium - demanding

Live in the Upper Calder Valley and fancy a pint at the Black Bull in Haworth? Or feel like pretending you're Catherine Earnshaw in black bonnet, taffeta and clogs, wafting in and out of the mists? Or would you simply like a day soaking up Brontë family history immersed among their environs? Or potter in the Apothecary? Then there's only one path to take: the Pennine Way! On a day to Haworth, the history, literature and landscape of which we Far-West Yorksians (born or adoptive) can be so proud will soften the hardest of over-stressed and under-exercised hearts.

At the end of this first series of walks, you'll be feeling fighting fit, I trust, and not letting a little matter of bleak weather or a long distance deter you, especially if you take sensible measures. This is a very straightforward walk (take a look at the OS South Pennines map) but it is indeed quite long, possibly wet and probably windy. It gives you scenery to cry for, but it's not the faint-hearted. And should you wish to return on foot as well, then an early start (especially in the winter months) is essential. If you prefer to return on the top of the 500 bus over the moors, you'll get wonderful views over to the very ridges and hills you tramped to get there. It's a thoroughly rewarding day out either way.

This time, as it's a long walk, it would be advisable to let someone know where you have gone and when you expect to be back; and/or have a mobile telephone with you.

A   Leaving Midgehole NT carpark, enter Hardcastle Crags and take the main estate road straight ahead of you. Twenty minutes' brisk walking will bring you to Gibson Mill. Continuing upwards, a further twenty minutes will take you high uphill out of the Crags onto the Shackleton-Walshaw road. Turn left onto this road.

B   After about 400 metres, you will reach the hamlet of Walshaw, now familiar to most of you. From the centre of the circle of houses, turn sharp right, following the signpost to Walshaw and Haworth. The road upwards bears left; before it reaches the farmhouse ahead of you, turn right up a short bank to a farm gate, at a signpost to Walshaw Dean. Then carry straight on up the hill, with a plantation to your left and the hills of Horodiddle on your right. Go over a stile at a gate at the top and follow the path - first left and then right - onto the clear moorland track called Dean Gate. Expansive views over to Lancashire will open up before you; curlews and grouse will chortle and circle around you; and over the hill the waters of Walshaw Dean reservoirs will tantalise you. Follow the path down towards the eastern bank, passing a shooting butt: a good place to stop and stoke up with a little refreshment and contemplate the gentle blue waters before you.

C   Near the bottom of the hill, fork right and head down to the dams. Turn right at the bottom and make your way along the eastern bank of the middle reservoir until - 300 yards later - you pass through a gate now taking you uphill and away from the water. At a signpost some 50 metres further on, bear right onto the Pennine Way. Though steep and a little boggy at first, this path soon becomes flag-stoned so that, for your safety, you have only to stick to the path for a fabulously exhilarating trek over the true tops of West Yorkshire. You will be completely blown away (only metaphorically speaking, one hopes) when you breast the crest and spy the peaks of North Yorkshire and even Cumbria on the skyline.

D   The flagged path will now lead you down to the rather sad remnants of Top Withens farmhouse where you must stop. The sheep expect it of you and would be terribly hurt if you just passed on without allowing them at least a sniff at your food bags. The ghost of the former Georgian inhabitants also expect a little homage, and - if you have any faith in the legend that this once fine farmhouse is indeed 'Wuthering Heights' - you might be lucky enough to feel the spirit of Emily skittering in and out of the shadows, cowering in cloak and with skirts a-swirling. Other walkers traditionally swap sandwiches and tall tales here; it's quite a social mecca. If for no other reason, a stop here is a chance to soak up the marvellous views over to and beyond Destination Haworth.

E   **Don't let the grass grow under your feet, though. Make it a sensibly short rest at Top Withens, and then set off down the hill towards Haworth.** After about 150 metres, turn right at the fork in the paths (the left branch leading you to Stanbury) and head down into the valley towards the Brontë Falls; you wind gently down until, after a stile, you stand high above the Falls and are then lured down the steep, rocky path to the bridge at the Falls. This is another favourite stopping place of great beauty and literary imaginings, but it has been known for ill-tempered sheep to chase you off the bridge if they're in threatened mood, so keep an eye on your bottom.

Cross the bridge, turn left and follow the rocky path out of the Falls; it joins a muddy farm track for the next half mile or so, until you reach Moor Side Lane with Penistone Hill ahead of you. Beware of fast-hurtling traffic as you cross the road.

F   **From Moor Side Lane, take any of the obvious north-bound pathways around to the left of Penistone Hill for about half a mile until you reach a smaller east-west-running road.** Cross over it, then follow a walled path straight ahead of you and down a short hill. Turn left at the bottom and you will find yourself - believe it or not - on a section of the Old Oxenhope Road (with a visitors' carpark and then animal pens on your right), thankfully approaching Haworth churchyard. As you squeeze through the gate, you pass into the home of the Brontës, the church of their father and the last resting-place of countless local tuberculosis victims. It is a poignant place. Visit either the church or the parsonage to gain an insight into the darker history of this community - which will both chill and inspire you and give a richer vein to your experience of the village as you wander past its tiny cottages where lives once thrived and so soon withered. And don't forget a sobering pint at the Black Bull where Branwell would morosely drink and besmirch the family's reputation gallon by gallon. Sit and quietly ponder: you got here on Shanks's pony and now you have climbed off it into picturesque history. What a complete experience!

Return either by taking the 500 bus from opposite Haworth Old Hall hotel (at the bottom of the High Street): buses leave at 1229, 1434, *1534 (*Saturdays only) and 1734. Be there or be stuck. Or (using the OS South Pennines map and taking the more easterly stretch of the Haworth-to-Hebden Bridge Walk, and doing so **only** if you've set off early enough to assure yourself of three or four more hours of daylight), walk back:

A: Penistone Hill to Leeshaw Reservoir

B: Leeshaw Reservoir to Grain Water Bridge (at the junction with the Old Haworth Road)

C: Grain Water Bridge through Coppy and Nook down to the NT carpark at Midgehole.

I've so enjoyed taking into the nooks and crannies of our region these last twelve walks. In the following twelve, I will be counting on your new hardiness and fitness so that I can offer you a more 'experienced' level of walks, so keep practising and then - read on.

FURTHER AFIELD

12 WALKS WHICH TAKE YOU BEYOND THE UPPER CALDER VALLEY BOOTS ON! WE'RE OFF AGAIN.

No rest for the walker! Let's be off again!

Now that you know your immediate environs so much better after the first series of walks, it's time to go further afield and conquer a wider radius of your beautiful and historic county. In this second series of twelve walks, you will sometimes be led right out of the West Riding, in fact, and end up in Lancashire - onto the Pennine Way, the Pendle Way, the Burnley Way and the Brontë Way. Truly breathtaking landscapes lie ahead to broaden your horizons. Most of them will take you very high so that you can see your world from a whole new perspective and come home able to keep life's problems in better proportion. Up on the summits, you'll be gob-smacked, wind-smacked and - if you have a hearty friend with you - back-slapped too.

Now that you're a more experienced walker, having already met many types of terrain in many types of weather, you'll by now be aware of the need for a well-equipped kit to carry on your back, and sound, weatherproof clothing. The smallest thing (such as slipping on mossy cobbles) can stop you in your tracks, which then - by virtue of the distance and time involved to either self-recover or get help - can mean a long wait: a wet, cold, hungry, lonely, dark wait - so take the trouble to have your walking rucksack always at the ready at home and try not to remove things from it - so that its contents will cover all contingencies and emergencies.

In your rucksack, you should always carry:

→ your mobile phone
→ whistle
→ torch
→ map (South Pennine Outdoor Leisure map 21)
→ compass
→ first aid kit
→ food (dry rations e.g. chocolate)
→ drink (a warm flask and water)
→ binoculars and/or camera.

Your should either wear or keep in your rucksack:

→ a woolly, ear-flapped hat
→ gloves
→ cagoule
→ boots
→ gaiters
→ walking stick
→ waterproof trousers
→ spare socks
→ extra clothing (spare tracksuit trousers and pullover).

That's not much, is it? It is a tidy amount that can easily be crammed into your average day-pack (a sensible one is usually between 25 and 35 litres' capacity and is strong) and will make you a lot safer and more secure. The number of times I've turned thankfully in at my door after a daily constitutional, looking forward to a warm welcome and a whisky, only to be met by a sharp dressing-down because I had forgotten to take my mobile with me! So try to remember everything.

Again, all the walks in this section of the book are circular. This can be reassuring to you and to those at home because you are less likely to try detours and you are aiming ultimately for your car, pub, bus stop or railway station. These aren't just 'muck about' walks; they can be remote and potentially dangerous - as all moorland terrains can be - so please heed the following precautions:

→ Keep children alert to their goals and unreliable dogs on a lead.
→ Watch your step. Stick to main tracks.
→ Beware of bogs. Avoid walking on bog cotton and stick to reedy tussocks.
→ Let someone know where you are going, when you expect to be back and where you will park your car.
→ Try not to go alone.
→ Keep moving briskly to maintain warmth, circulation and schedule.
→ Don't dawdle, but neither should you hurry over uneven ground. To appreciate views, stop fully and briefly.
→ Select the best daylight hours: in winter, set off early. In wet, cold conditions, don't go off at tangents; stick to your plans.
→ Don't do anything silly, like trying to scale unscheduled rocks or clear a clough in one bound.

I may be making it sound as if you're off to bag a couple of dozen Munros or to do the Pennine Way from start to finish, but anyone's experience will tell you that it's all wise advice.

But be cheerful! You're fit, your complexion is already weathering (if not wizening) nicely from all your recent walking experiences and you're rearing to go! You'll be given, where applicable, bus and train numbers and nearest stops to your start/finish point, plus some timetable information; these will be current at time of going to press, but should you attempt one of these walks some months after buying this book, you should rely on your own double-checking.

Grid references from the South Pennines Outdoor Leisure map 21 are once again provided for the convenience of those who know how to read such things. If you don't, find out and search your walk area on paper before you set off. Distances are quite long so check the tread on your boots and, if the soles are severely worn down, consider buying a new pair.

So come with me now on some truly fascinating journeys - and prepare for the heady reward of saying that you did them all under excellent guidance and on your own two feet.

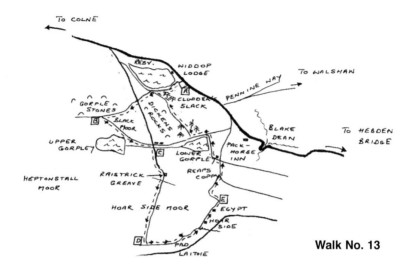

Walk No. 13

YOUR ROUTE: - - ⟶ - -

START AND END AT [A]

72

WALK NO. 13

EGYPT AND BACK IN TIME FOR TEA

Widdop Lodge (GR958314) - Gorple Gate - Clegg Clough
- Egypt - Reaps Coppy - **Widdop Lodge**

Distance: 7.75 miles (12.5 km). Leave 4-5 hours
Conditions: Generally good; boggy and muddy in places
Level: Medium - demanding; two steep ascents

Want to see the wonders of Egypt and be back in time for tea? Stand grand on granite stones and entranced on mountainous outcrops with three 'seas' of blue water to dazzle you - and still end up with your hands wrapped around a pint of Yorkshire ale? Well, you can! Come on this walk which takes you from Gorple Stones through to gorgeous Noahdale and all this will be yours. You'll travel through broad, eye-opening country, all without the need for a passport!

There is no bus as far out as Widdop, so a car (or in finer weather a bicycle) will be needed to get you to the starting point. Widdop lies seven miles and fifteen minutes' drive from Hebden Bridge or Todmorden.

A **From the carpark at Widdop Lodge, set off west along the cobbled wall of Widdop Reservoir** with the imposing rocks of Cludders Slack bearing down over you. Once over the water, turn right and follow the track past a small pine plantation (where cuckoos chant in spring) to take you, after about 800 metres, uphill away from the water. It is quite a stiff climb up and into the hill, but you can take a breather when you reach the junction of your path with the Burnley Way: take in the views back over to Widdop and Walshaw which are so reminiscent of Scottish glens. Turn left at this point, continuing up and over the hill to Gorple Gate where the track opens out onto a glorious hilltop with Gorple Upper Reservoir in the near distance.

B **Bear left and head down towards Gorple Lower Reservoir, ignoring for today the signpost to Worsley (a branch of the Burnley Way).** Stop briefly to clamber onto the fabulous Gorple Stones and take in the views over the reservoir and countryside beyond. Then jump back onto the path down via Black Moor to Gorple Upper Reservoir. Eastwards, towards Gorple Lower, you can see round the bend to Blake Dean, a comforting sight as, close at hand, it's quite lonely with hardly even a sheep, but the paths are clear and well laid-out to make you feel safe, quite important if you are on your own.

At the bottom of the hill, with the reservoir now facing you, turn left onto a concreted track and saunter down past a pine plantation on your right, with Reaps Water burbling away beyond it. The water of Gorple Lower now glistens before you (are you keeping up with all these Gorples?) and Dickens Rocks on your left form a fine corridor of handsomeness.

C   Quite soon, you reach grouse butts on your left. Here a grassy path on your right will drop down the bank and lead you over towards Reaps Water. Here too you will find the first of the trusty yellow arrows of the Calderdale Countryside Service, a series of which will guide your way over this bare and boggy moor. Now heading due south, cross a plank over the water, and the terrain will immediately become more rugged as you begin to make your way over Heptonstall Moor, so have your walking stick at the ready.

You are going against a stream valley (Clegg Clough) and it's all tussock and bog for a while. Up on the rise, the CCS has laid down some nice slabs to make it all a bit more passable. Soon you will see on the rise a Brontë-esque farmhouse - the empty shell of Raistrick Greave. Follow the path towards it; it will pull you in for a while, its sixteenth-century ghosts demanding a little of your time and company. Once you have humoured them, take the right-hand path out of the far enclosure, picking your way carefully over the rocks and bog, and climb up the hill until you reach a water channel: turn left and follow the channel to a culvert over the stream. Cross over and mount the hill, still bearing south. Following the CCS signs all the way, you will find yourself on Hoar Side Moor and, as you breast the crest of the moor, you will see in the distance the farmhouses of Widdop, the hills of Hardcastle Crags and even Pecket Well. At eye-level, you are in the safe hands of home, but underfoot, beware unfriendly terrain! You still have about half a mile to go of soggy, boggy moor and stream-banks which will demand your keenest attention.

When you reach an east-west fenceline barring your continued progress south, turn left (at the arrow) and begin to make your way to Egypt. You are now in Noahdale, the once-thriving valley of hand-loom weavers and their families, and the watery conditions might make you feel a bit biblical yourself!

D   But you're not out of the bog yet. The first field into Noahdale is quite difficult. Once you reach a stile, go over it and down a walled track leading you to Colden Water. The dismantled farmhouse of Pad Laithe is now inhabited only by the cattle who feed there. Struggle down the muddy track until it reaches the bottom: you have the shell of Colden Water farmhouse at your left shoulder and a footbridge across the water (towards Blackshaw Head) on your right, but carry straight on, through a metal gate and up the short bank to the distinctly inhabited Hoar Side farmhouse, yet another of the edifices which used to house weavers who contributed to the former prosperity of this valley. Stay on the track around to the left of the farmhouse (you can now see around into Colden Valley) until you reach Rough Hey, followed by the handsome Egypt Farm. All these farmhouses were once within the town boundaries of Heptonstall and were a major source of its pride.

E   Go through the gate at Egypt and turn left, back up over the hill towards Reaps Coppy; you are now on the last leg back to Widdop. The views over to Blake Dean as you come over the hill are truly magnificent in any season, *and* if it's bright and sunny, it's Far-West Yorkshire at its most boastful. The Packhorse Inn also gleams at you, reminding you to drop in for a pint on your way back in the car.

At the bottom of the hill, go through the gate and over the water channel; turn left past the Gorple Cottages and right onto the causeway of the reservoir. A rich contrast from the land-locked moors you were on an hour ago, here the water will blow its vapour in your face and all your last cobwebs away. At the end of the causeway, turn left again and tramp along the road for about 400 metres (now in the direction of Gorple Upper), but keep an eye on the two pine plantations on your right. Your last path will take you up between the groups of trees and back over the hill to Widdop. Pass a disused quarry on your left and, just before a little bridge over a stream, cut up to your right over a little grassy bank. Be advised that the hill is quite steep and it gets boggier towards the top.

Near the top at Cludders Slack, prepare for a really dramatic vista: your final destination lies tantalisingly close and, as you reach the crest, Widdop and its waters welcome you with wide open arms: gulls, grouse and curlews sing, water ripples, the odd distant car slides silently along the top road - and otherwise all else should be silent (unless a bunch of climbers are out and over-excited: the fabulous stones along to your left are favourite haunt of abseilers, rock climbers and the Rescue Team). What a majestic view-point: real king-of-the-castle stuff. Where else in the world would you want to be?

Now cease this romantic entrancement and head down carefully, the path leading you back towards the pine plantation, past the boulders so attractively littering the hillside and then onto the track west of the reservoir and back to the carpark, tired no doubt but smiling and exhilarated, I'll bet. Now don't forget the Packhorse: it needs watering.

Walk No. 14

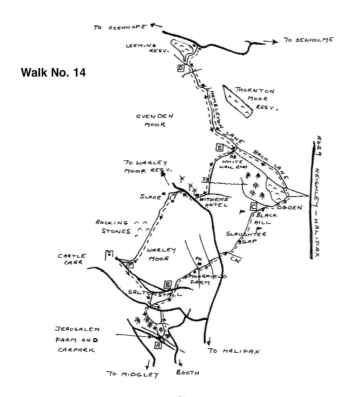

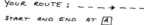

YOUR ROUTE : – – – → – – –
START AND END AT [A]

77

WALK NO. 14

AND DID THOSE JERUSALEM FEET?

Jerusalem Farm (GR037278) - *Upper Saltonstall - Slaughter Gap - Black Hill - Ogden - Oxenhope - Cold Edge - Rocking Stones - Jerusalem Farm*

Distance: 11.25 miles (18 km). Leave 5-6 hours
Conditions: Generally excellent; one boggy field
Level: Medium - demanding: long distance; a steep ascent

This is a day-long walk: for a fine, dry day offering dramatic variations of terrain such as you might only expect to see in, say, Scandinavia: green woodland, cosy farmland, open moorland, pine plantations, bubbling brooks and - of course - the mandatory peat bog!

You can catch a bus from Halifax (574 or 575) to Booth (often displayed to Midgley) which takes you almost as far as Jerusalem Lane (ask the driver). Conversely, there is an adequate, free carpark at Jerusalem Farm, where you can also let someone know of your itinerary.

A   **From the carpark, drop through the gate and down the grassy lane to the stone footbridge over Luddenden Dean. Bear right away from the brook** and make your way up through the leafy woods until you meet a gate and a signpost to Saltonstall. Walk straight up the hill before you to take you onto the Saltonstall Road. Turn left here and saunter into the tiny hamlet of Upper Saltonstall. After about 250 yards past a couple of farmhouses, turn right up a track signed first to the Calderdale Way, take the stile into a tussocky field, and walk east towards Wainstalls.

B   **The field brings you out now at the fork in two 'roads' (one the Upper Saltonstall Lane, the other leading to Warley). Cross over both** (watching for traffic), bear slightly right and follow the CW signpost onto the moor. Go over a stile and head, more or less parallel to the Wainstalls-Warley road, towards Moorfields Farm, its windbreak of trees being your guide.

Over a stile at the farm, emerge onto a farm track and cross into the courtyard of the Old Moorcock pub, from which you are led through a gate into a horse field: continue over stiles and down a flagged path towards a gate onto yet another farm lane. Turn left here for 15 yards until a gap in the stone wall on your right directs you into a second horse field, over a tiny stream and up through a cattle field to a ladder-stile. Head up towards a farmhouse, skirt around the left-hand side of the house, and emerge onto the Halifax-Ovenden Moor road.

Turn left and walk along the road for only 25 yards, then turn right (onto the Calderdale Way for a wee while) to be led gently down between tumbled-down walls (and ignoring the CW signpost which would lure you right), bearing left towards Ogden Plantation and Water. At this stage beautiful views of the valleys of Illingworth and Bradshaw swim into your ken.

You pass Slaughter Gap where two walls meet at a clough which falls away down the hill towards Mixenden Reservoir. Continue to bear left over the hill, heading for Mixenden Ings golf course and Black Hill beyond. Once over a stile and onto the fairway (watching for flying balls from the right), head up the hill facing you and through shoulder-deep gorse and bracken. Emerge at the top of Black Hill and walk straight ahead towards the trees of Ogden Plantation.

C   **Once out of the golf course land, turn right at the cement path which borders the Plantation and head down the hill towards the Water at the bottom.** Cross the causeway (pausing, of course, to appreciate the refreshing blueness of the Water), then head up the hill past the Visitor Centre, bearing left where the road and carpark entrances meet. Take a sharp left through the lower carpark and, at its end, go through a gate. After about 500 yards, you are out in open country once again, on a path called Back Lane and heading virtually straight ahead (northwest) towards the wind farm. A deep clough - the famous White Wall End at Great Scar - now gapes at you from the left as you follow the broad, sandy path above it which now becomes Hambleton Lane, once an ancient trading route. As you reach its crest, you are given gorgeous views north: Thornton Moor Reservoir and Leeming Reservoir in the foreground, Keighley and Bingley in the middle distance, and North Yorkshire and its undulations beyond.

Soon a signpost bearing a blue arrow (indicating the Brontë Way and Millennium Path) will lead you left down the grassy hill to Leeming Reservoir and Oxenhope.   Interrupting your downward amble, a ladder-stile guides you safely over the Great Conduit; at the bottom, go right through a pretty glade which leads you around the top of the reservoir, and follow the path up to the Oxenhope Road (B6141). Now choose with some difficulty: will it be right to The Dog and Gun, or left to The Lamb? Either decision means a further ten-minute walk. (If you are really tired and at the end of your leg-power, you can await the services of the 500 bus from Oxenhope to return you over the moors to Hebden Bridge or Todmorden [an hourly service at most times; enquire at the Post Office] - or, if you are still full of beans and it is a lovely day, then do walk back.)

D   You return via exactly the same route until you reach White Wall End. Here go down the steep steps to the clough, over the footbridge, then up again, not forgetting to turn and take in the gorgeous views down through the ravine towards Halifax. Go over the stile and take the path out of the clough (westwards above Skirden Clough) which will coax you once again under the wings of the wind turbines. After about half a mile, at a T-junction, turn right towards the famous Withens Hotel. Tarry over a well-deserved ale or two (especially if you abstained at Oxenhope), then turn briskly right onto Cold End Road, being particularly careful of fast-moving traffic as it heads to and from the reservoirs and wind farm.

E   Just opposite the carpark for the wind farm, turn left down onto a track towards Withens Head Farm and Slade Farm. As you look towards the farmhouse you will be delighted by your first view for the day of Stoodley Pike beyond. Persist with the tricky path around the latter farm, then follow the track towards the rocky outcrop of Rocking Stones, already visible ahead of you. You are crossing the heart of Warley Moor and you are at your wildest for the day; but it can be very boggy on this stretch and you may be glad of your gaiters! Soon a clearer path through heather opens up and you will find yourself virtually rolling towards the expansive, embracing valley of Luddenden Dean.

F   Say goodbye to the moorlands and climb over the stile onto the road. You are at the 'end of the line': at Mr Carr's famous castellated gatehouse marking the boundary of the Castle Carr Estate. Turn left and walk along the road for about 350 yards, then fork right and wind down to Upper Saltonstall; when you hit the road at the houses, turn right this time (instead of the expected left) and follow the road round for 100 yards to the Public Footpath sign at 'The Hunnet'. Take the grassy path down between the farmhouse and cow-paddock; you are now in earshot of the waters of Luddenden Dean and you have a comforting short amble through the Ridings fields into Jerusalem Farm woods once again, back to the bridge and carpark.

This has been our longest walk yet so you are no doubt tired and a little foot-sore. Why not bathe your feet in the waters of the Dean and relax on its grassy banks before heading back to the vehicle, and self-congratulate that you have covered in one day so much of wonderful Calderdale. Well done!

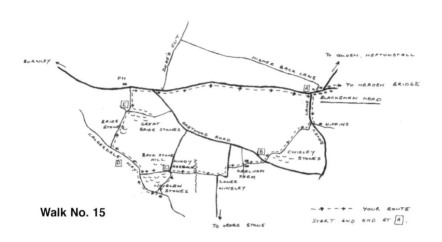

Walk No. 15

WALK NO. 15

ROCK OFF THE EXCESS POUNDS

Blackshaw Head (GR037278) - Chisley Stones
- Whirlaw Stones - Great Bride Stones - Blackshaw Head

Distance: 5.25 miles (9 km). Leave 3-4 hours
Conditions: Generally excellent; one boggy path
Level: Easy - medium

Here's a walk to have you clambering sprightly and literally jumping with life. It takes in at least three sets of impressive rocks, accessed via some gentle hillside lanes which traverse rather than climb the heights, so it's not too vertical: easily manageable by all mobile members of the family, plus the dog.

Choose a peerless blue day so that the views from each of the sets of rocks are taken in to best advantage. Set off from and return to Blackshaw Head: there is a bus from Hebden Bridge or Todmorden, or, if you want to extend the pleasure (and the exertion), you could walk up from the A646 at Charlestown by climbing through Jumble Hole Clough (see Walk no. 3) and emerging at Hippins.

A   At Blackshaw Head road junction, facing east, turn first left down Davey Lane and descend the hill as far as the bridge at Hippins (this is where Jumble Hole walkers will start). The handsome seventeenth-century farmhouse will be your landmark. Peel right off the road onto a signed path which takes you first up the hill, then along a straight culvert, then up over the heather to Chisley Stones. These are pleasing rocks, worthy of a tiny exploration and a 'king of the castle' game; do stop long enough to appreciate the fantastic views already opening up to the south. Then continue south beyond the stones and into a sheep field, and emerge onto Eastwood Road.

B   Turn right onto Eastwood Road and cross into the fields towards Keelham Farm. Follow the path to the right of the farmhouse onto Keelham Lane and turn left, heading down the hill towards Lower Winsley Farm. You will be led onto the Cross Stone road: wind down it for about 100 yards until you meet a broad bridleway to the right of the road. This attractive path traverses the hill and takes you into a pretty clough typical of our area: trees and walls and water - and mud, of course. The path will lead you up along the ridge to Windy Harbour Lane.

C At Windy Harbour Lane, turn immediately left into a field and wind down a rough track towards East and West Whirlaw. The fine upstanding Whirlaw Stones are on your right, but you are not encouraged to cross them (and the farmer, if he sees you, might well shout out the correct directions for you) but to head to the bottom and get firmly onto the Calderdale Way. Go right at West Whirlaw and skirt the imposing Whirlaw Common Hill, keeping to the flagstones of the CW. Should you be feeling a bit deprived and peeved, you could cut up the slope at Back Stone Hill (to your right) and grab the view from the top of the Stones and then return to the path.

D Remain on the Calderdale Way, now heading northeast, and where the CW path forks (and not following it down to the left), go through a gate and dart up to the Golden Stones for yet another breathtaking view. Follow the path up via Bride Stones to reach Great Bride Stones, no doubt already exhilarated and sated with beauty. But this is now the dramatic climax to your walk as you clamber onto the rocks and take in the fabulous views. Take your time here and indulge in the antiquity and the strength of these marvellous pillars of grit, as well as in the vantage point you have over the South Pennines: the views are at least 180 degrees and you can see Lancashire in particular at its very handsomest. It's also a good place to stop for refreshment and play. The children and the dog will need to be watched carefully, however, as it is easy to slip on the smooth, often wet rocks or to disappear temporarily from view.

E When you've taken your fill of beauty and the 'buzz', cross Bride Stones Moor heading north, emerge onto the Blackshaw Head road and turn right and walk along the road - keeping safely to the right - as far as Dukes Cut on the left (not the most attractive or welcoming track in the world but useful access): after a good three or four hundred metres, a turn on your right will take you onto Higher

Back Lane and give you a more interesting route, across fields rather than tarmac, back into Blackshaw Head. If you're still fit for even more fancy footwork, consider heading into Hebden Bridge via Jacks Bridge (where the new delights at the New Delight are worth a try) and Ragley Lane (see Walk no. 3), feeling elated, I hope, and well and

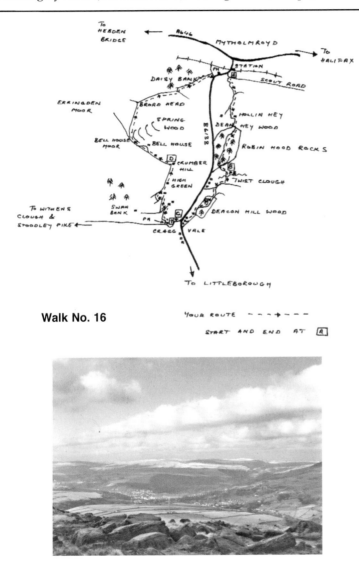

Walk No. 16

YOUR ROUTE - - - ↠ - - -

START AND END AT [A]

truly 'stoned'.

WALK NO. 16

HISTORY AND BEAUTY ABOVE
MODERN MYTHOLMROYD

Mytholmroyd Station (GR01325) - Dean Hey Woods
- Deacon Hill Woods - Bell House Moor - Daisy Bank - Mytholmroyd

Distance: 6.5 miles (10 km.) Leave 4 hours
Conditions: Wet and boggy in two areas; two steep ascents
Level: Medium - hard

This walk offers an enormous breadth of topographical experiences: from woodland and fields to ridges and moors, but it also takes in an historic hamlet and both elegant and 'notorious' stone houses which put the stamp of 'Endurance' on our well-earthed valley: and all within no more than a mile or so in any direction out of Mytholmroyd. While it offers very varied beauty, it is seldom a dry walk, however, either under the cover of the woods or out on the open moors, so you will need to be prepared to watch your step as well as to watch the changes of scenery.

Against bad conditions, may I urge you to have your best boots (and even gaiters) on you, and to rely on the support of both a walking stick and the arm or two of a good friend. If alone, it would be wise to have your mobile with you. Don't let me alarm you, but even within a small ambit, uneven, boggy or sloping ground can magnetically attract ankles and have you over in a microsecond.

A   **At the Mytholmroyd Railway Station bridge, turn south to face Cragg Vale and walk along the pavement up to the Scout Road junction.** Turn left into the road and then immediately right at the chapel up into Hall Bank Lane. Head steeply uphill at first, past houses and farmhouses, after which the track opens out onto broad fields. More gentle climbing will find you at Hollin Hey Farm; head towards the line of trees marking the northern boundary of Dean Hey Woods. Drop gently down through the woods, where the path becomes very wet at times as streams from the Robin Hood Rocks above you trickle - or sometimes gush - across your path. (You are discreetly hidden away from the Cragg Vale road which runs parallel to you a little to the east.) At the southernmost boundary wall of the woods, you will emerge into more open countryside at Glen House, above Twist Clough.

B   Bear left out of the woods and uphill, so that you are climbing above the pretty, deep valley of Twist Clough. A footbridge will take you across the water on the southern side of the valley to meet a farm track. Go right (downhill now) at first, then wind back to the left past a handful of houses, and pick your way into Deacon Hill Wood. (Use the map very closely here, and find the path into the middle of the woods; do not attempt the path above the woods, as a false footing or a momentary lapse in concentration could see you dropping through one of the heather-concealed 'holes' in the bank and sliding down the hill.) Once again, woodland offers you a most attractive sylvan experience with ancient trees giving a glorious roof. Head out of these smaller woods at Church Bank and walk down past some houses onto the B6138 at Cragg Vale.

C   Cross the road here and walk down into the hamlet of the Vale, past the charming ancient church and into the dell of Cragg. (The Hinchliffe Arms is always most welcoming to the walker, and I suggest a warm of the feet and a dry-off of the socks over a pint of Landlord's, as long as you don't dally too long and forget the climbs and moorland bogs still ahead of you.) Turn first right after the pub and head up past the handsome cluster of dwellings at Old Cragg Hall, and zigzag steeply to the top of the hill near Swan Bank. Go left past some ramshackle farm buildings, then bear right and head northeast along a broad, straight farm track past High Green to a sharp left-hand turn at Crumber Hill 'corner'. Turn left onto the last piece of track before you hit the Bell House and Erringden moors.

D   You are now entering Coiners' territory: the house of David Hartley, the eighteenth-century counterfeiter - known locally as 'King David' - is the second house you come to. You will notice that it is a compact little place. It was here, no doubt, that countless 'new' coins melted from the clipped edges of real ones were stored for later trading. True to the murky atmosphere of the place, the path past

Keelham now becomes increasingly boggy as you navigate the area which sits just above the glorious gorge of Broad Head Clough, so do tread carefully. If you can, avoid 'broadening' the path by skirting the bog and thereby being responsible for initiating further erosion; stick as close as you can to the centre of the sludge, without getting in it up to your knees, of course. (If you venture into the grasses, be advised that water lurks beneath and that you should only move the next foot when the first is firmly lodged on a tussock.) This soggy moor is best suited to only healthy ankles. David Hartley was no fool; I guess he knew no one much would trouble him up in these hazardous parts.

E   **When you can afford to look up, you will see that you are venturing onto the higher moor of Erringden** and that the views over to Midgley Moor and over to Warley are most impressive. Beyond Broad Head - where you should stop and gaze at the mystery of the wood Spring-ing out of the sheer walls of the Clough - you will scale a couple of stiles, then veer right at a newish pine plantation and head down Daisy Bank into Mytholmroyd. Steer right at the bottom into Nest Lane, then left into Stocks Lane for the station via, perhaps, the Shoulder of Mutton. It's been a taxing walk with masses of rewards: let a pint be another!

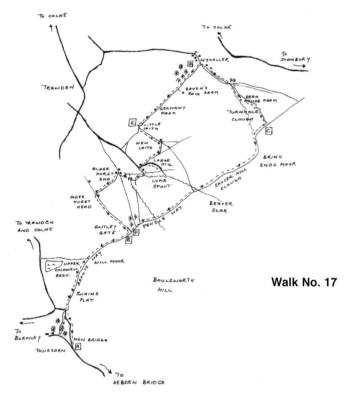

Walk No. 17

WALK NO. 17

WONDROUS WYCOLLER AND
WATERFALLS BEYOND

Thursden (GR905348) - Will Moor - Brinks End - Wycoller
- Little Laith - Alder Hurst End - Antley Gate - Thursden

Distance: 8.25 miles (13 km). Leave 4 - 5 hours
Conditions: Generally excellent
Level: Medium

Let's walk to Wycoller in the spirit - if not the actual steps - of the Brontës, breasting their isolated moors, trekking the paths they surely knew and arriving at a haven of their Victorian gentility. We will walk from the present into the past and from the edges of industrial Lancashire into their more barren Yorkshire rurality.

Wycoller was once a thriving community, the estate of the influential Cunliffe family where farmers and weavers prospered. But the village emptied after the Industrial Revolution when production migrated to the large mill towns. Afterwards, when various Water Board schemes for the village came to nothing, it became a popular country park; it now welcomes visitors to its stone bridges, aisled barn and pretty beck - and to its excellent café - and you can sit and ponder or picnic in the lea of Wycoller Hall: the model for Charlotte Brontë's 'Ferndean Manor' where Jane Eyre finally found her Mr Rochester.

This particular Wycoller walk begins - I regret to say - where no bus goes: near Thursden. Driving from Hebden Bridge or Todmorden, head out beyond Widdop Reservoir and park your car at the steep 'turning circle' near the cattle-grid at New Bridge: just where the narrow road turns up towards Colne. (Only the most ridiculously fit person might cycle to the starting point; I dare say there are some among us who will.)

A   At New Bridge, walk north up the steep road for about 400 metres, passing the signpost to the Brontë Way. Bear right at the top of the road, just before the junction, and head towards a gate which leads onto the moors. Within a hundred metres or so, you will reach an ancient stone doorway standing all by itself at Swains Plat whose beauty and history will demand your reflection for a few moments. This ancient dwelling then points your way down to the junction with the Pendle Way, where the path from the Coldwell Reservoirs (west) meets yours.

B **Now the path becomes broad and easy, affording you fabulous views of Boulsworth Hill and taking you past the prosperous farms which edge Will Moor.** **You are walking securely northeast now:** past Boulsworth Dyke towards Brinks Ends Moor, and bypassing the majestic yet controversial 'Hill' - which you can, for now, do no more than admire. It is the highest point in the South Pennines (1696 feet) and was in recent years the subject of a 'mass trespass' by the Ramblers' Association. Much of the area remains out of bounds and is the preserve of the Water Authority, but greater access is constantly sought and hopefully more likely as time goes on.

C **Near Brink Ends Moor, you skirt Beaver Scar and Saucer Hill Clough to your right,** which are dramatic minions of the Hill and are shadowed right down into the becks by its giant strength; their rocks hurled helter-skelter, the Scar and the Clough thunder with water at most times of the year. From your path, you now drop down into the more modest Turnhole Clough and cross over the beck; then at the signpost on the rise, turn left onto the Brontë Way once more. Saunter over the fields and hillocks, through Dean House Farm, and then follow the single-track road beside the water into Wycoller.

D **Soak up your fill of Wycoller's small delights** (such as the Hall, the café and the water under the packhorse bridge; fling stones into it and make wishes and admire the halcyon quietude of the hamlet), then walk back towards the stone-slabbed bridge opposite Wycoller Hall. Cross the beck and head up a steep farm track, through a young plantation and out into the fields at Ravens Rock Farm. You are now in walled fields, crossed at regular intervals by stiles and puddles. Your path now lies straight ahead, past a farm or two: Germany Farm and Little Laith Farm. At this stage, the terrain is so benign you could be in the Home Counties, but never fear: raw Yorkshire lies safely ahead of you, and Pendle Hill looms to the west.

E   At Little Laith Farm, go left and cross the field to New Laith, then head southwest again down the farm 'drive' towards Lodge Hill. Hitting the tarmac, you pass a collection of pretty cottages where you turn right and walk through Lodge Hill Farm, down a hill towards the waterfalls of Lumb Spout (similar - but perhaps superior - to Lumb Falls) with its peaceful summer bathing holes and perfect privacy. It is an idyllic spot, so loiter here if you will. From the falls, climb up onto the farm road at Alder Hurst End. Turn right onto it, then left onto a straight, well-surfaced track to Alder Hurst Head farmhouse. Behind the farmhouse, pick up the path through the boggier terrain that takes you to Antley Gate.

F   At Antley Gate, rejoin the Pendle Way and retrace your steps over Will Moor back onto the Brontë Way and return either via the road or the pine woods to New Bridge, contemplating not only your enchanting walk of history and beauty, but also your return to the car and how sad - or relieved - you'll be to succumb once again to mere wheels. With your nearest pint at the Packhorse Inn calling, I guess I can understand how a car will hasten you there.

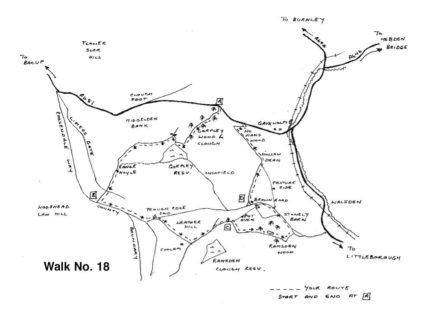

Walk No. 18

- - - - - YOUR ROUTE
START AND END AT A

WALK NO. 18

GORPLEY OFFERING TWO OF EVERYTHING

Gorpley Wood (GR919235) - Gorpley Reservoir
- Rossendale Way - Ramsden Clough Reservoir
- Ramsden Wood - No Mans Land - Gorpley Wood

Distance: 5.5 miles (9 km). Leave 3 - 3.5 hours
Conditions: Soft and often wet underfoot
Level: Medium

Two counties, two woods, two cloughs, two reservoirs! Two proud county pathways, two boots and two walking companions (one canine and the other merely human, perhaps?), a doubly rewarding walk and one which you might call a 'professional' walk: not such a pretty one as the last to Wycoller, yet deeply historic and tremendously dramatic at the same time. It takes you in the footsteps of the Limers who plied their goods between Lancashire and Yorkshire; it takes you up to the county boundary line where the ghosts of those who have scoured this terrain before you remain your inspiration; you clamber up onto the Rossendale Way and beam down upon the grandeur of the countryside: Stoodley Pike your faithful guide and the Pennine, Brontë, Calderdale and Rossendale Ways all in view and boasting their hills' wares. (Can't say I was thrilled to come down the other side into a marching line of power pylons, striding their way up and down the counties. But I suppose they have to be somewhere, so either ignore them or pity them: they're socially very isolated, poor things. I'm sure you won't let them spoil your fascinating walk.)

Conveniently there is a bus-stop - on the A681 Todmorden-to-Bacup road - just metres from your starting point; or park your car off the road about a mile east of the Gauxholme/Todmorden junction and railway bridge.

A   Off the A681 - just east of Clough Foot and where Midgelden Brook runs parallel to the road - a wooden signpost points southwest to your path up through Gorpley Wood. This section is both picturesque and majestic, taking you up through the pleasant clough and its waterfalls as far as Gorpley Reservoir. You emerge from the woods and onto more open hillside at the Water Plant where you bear right (west) up towards a farmhouse (despite barking guard dogs, you should be quite safe to walk between the farm buildings). Turn left onto a track which is the Calderdale Way link path and strike out onto the moors; this nice open ridge will lead you across some minor streams and up Range Hoyle Hill. You cross the top of the waterfalls and clough which fall into Gorpley Reservoir and, from here, the view back towards Todmorden is wonderful.

B **When you reach the ridge - after some pretty wet and stodgy climbing - you will be on the Rossendale Way and the county boundary.** Hogshead Law Hill looms up before you, and on a fine day you are afforded fabulous views into further Lancashire. Here too you will notice a huge 'mearstone' or two tossed casually about the ground with a deep-etched 'T' uppermost: just a reminder that this boundary once also marked off the Lancashire estate of the sixteenth-century landowner, Sir John Towneley of Towneley Hall, of whose four-hundred-year Burnley-based dynasty the area should be justly proud. Turn right (south) and bowl along the ridge, following the ancient stone wall on your right, and trudge the route of the ancient limers who quarried in this area and transported their wares from here into Yorkshire via the moorland ridges. Bear left (east) at Trough Edge End where you will find a fenced-off trig. Go through the gate here and head down the hill, past an eerie disused mine, the tumbledown farmhouse at Coolam and find yourself at Ramsden Clough Reservoir. The views as you descend are literally powerful, redolent of teeming eighteenth-century industry: quite grim and forbidding yet highly atmospheric.

C **At the bottom of the hill, turn left (east) and follow the track down beyond Ramsden Clough Reservoir and drop down, near Pot Oven, though the wooded pathways into Ramsden Wood.** This is a pretty walk back into the sylvan idiom with its waterfalls leading you steeply downhill. At the old mill chimneys, bear left again and head up via Stonely Barn and Brown Road to pick up the ancient, paved pathway signposted to Gauxholme. At this point, you have completed (from the Reservoir) two sides of a rough isosceles triangle, with Ramsden Wood having been a mere detour from the main path.

D   The next path is broad and open, heading you north now (towards Gauxholme); it is paved with ancient flagstones, and guides you safely across marshy ground, with Inchfield Pasture to your right. Ignoring the right-hand fork taking you to Gauxholme, keep straight ahead - with handsome Flower Scar Hill, a mile or two to the north, guiding your way - down past Hollow Dean Farm, through No Mans Land wood. Drop down once again back onto the A681 just 500 metres southeast of your bus-stop or carpark. Turn left and walk carefully back along the road to your starting point.

Most exhilarating, I'm sure you will agree, and very satisfying in that you seem to have seen double - without any discomfort or disorientation - all the way. With no pub in the immediate vicinity to reward you, why not have a well-earned thermos instead!

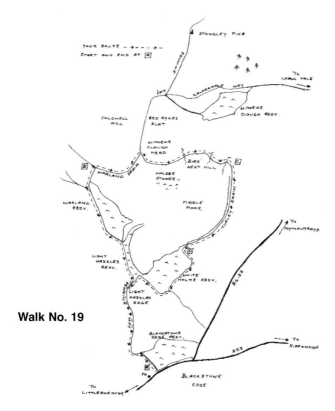

Walk No. 19

WALK NO. 19

THE RESERVOIR CIRCUIT

*Blackstone Edge (White House Inn) (GR969179) - Light Hazzles Edge - Turley Holes - White Holme - **White House Inn***

Distance: 7.5 miles (12.5 km). Leave 3 hours
Conditions: Generally excellent; soft and wet underfoot in parts
Level: Easy - medium

This walk has everything you could ask for: the thrill of the Pennine Way, broad views, flat ridges, water, firm conditions underfoot - and a pub at the end. Farther away, but seeming as close as the end of your arm, Pendle Hill (Lancashire) becomes your guide for the first part of the walk when the waters of the reservoirs lap close at your feet; and then it withdraws courtly to allow Stoodley Pike to step in, take over the rougher parts of the walk and escort you the rest of the way.

Either 'bus' it (the 900 bus between Ripponden and Hebden Bridge passes here four times a day between Monday and Saturday: check times before setting off) or drive (there are two large parking bays just west of the White House pub) to Blackstone Edge, and prepare to let yourself be gently drawn round the Reservoir Circuit. Because the Water Authority shares the responsibility for the pathways here, they are well maintained and vehicleworthy, and it is a pleasant 'sharing' experience for you as you take advantage of the flat, firm surfaces - for much of the way, at least.

A   Following the signpost pointing northeast, set off from the White House Inn onto the Pennine Way. You may have to navigate your way through a herd or two of cattle on the early stretches, but they will grudgingly let you through if you're gentle with them. Stride along the broad path which borders Light Hazzles Reservoir and takes you effortlessly to Warland Reservoir, with nothing (if you've picked a fine, sunny day) to impede your views northwest to Pendle Hill: an extraordinarily broad and distant vista, but you are already at 1000 feet above sea level, so panoramic views are understandable. Continue for a couple more north-going kilometres to the end-tip of Warland Reservoir. That's quite a lot of water you've had with you already, not unlike walking on a long coastal beach.

B   When the Pennine Way turns eastwards, you make a small climb out of the reservoir areas onto more uneven ground, as if heading for Red Dykes Flats and Coldwell Hill and pre-empting the bogginess still to come. The sudden foot-watching required may be something of an irritant after the easy walking so far but, as if to make amends, Stoodley Pike stands nobly at the ready to woo you further on. (But you shall have to admire from afar today, as we are turning off to let it follow us instead.) In the midst of the moor, fingerposts appear at wonderful Withens Clough Head; turn right onto what is signposted as the 'Reservoir Circuit to White Holme'. As you travel past the grand and imposing Holder Stones, do either stop to soak up the views or, better still, 'scamper' up to the rocks. From here the aspect over the Withens Reservoir is wonderful, or, if you simply swivel around on the path, you'll get a whole new take on Stoodley Pike, now retiring graciously but offering itself at a dramatic new angle beyond the Withens pine plantations and the fabulous rolls of hills. Return to the path and begin to take more care as you go past Bird Nest Hill, as fords and cloughs materialise on your right, and the ground is not only a little boggy here, but very black indeed, with the surface vegetation peeled away to expose the raw peat.

C   The path now bears south again as it begins to bring you full circle over Turley Holes and Higher House Moor. You now walk into the heart of Middle Moor in the most open of countryside, following feeder streams and less-established pathways, so expect wetness and do take care. A paved path ably assists you in this section, however: Turley Drain path taking you to White Holme Reservoir. On this lovely stretch, spring curlews and wagtails will herald your presence noisily. You are walking parallel to and high above the Cragg Vale Road (B6138), which you can see far below you, and with Soyland and Rishworth Moors just beyond to the southeast.

D   At White Holme Reservoir, wind around the waterside pathway of the reservoir and savour the watery breezes as they - almost invariably - blow in your face. Ignore the Authority road off to the left which would take you onto the B6138, and bear right (west), continuing your 'circle' back to Light Hazzles Edge, then left (south) once more, retracing your early steps onto the Pennine Way (and don't forget to thank the cows for the pleasure).

On top of the world? Close. High all the way? Definitely. And, at the end, your feet should be pain-free except for the itch to get out on another such gorgeous walk. Direct them instead to the White House pub, a fine alternative, especially if there's a long wait for the next bus home.

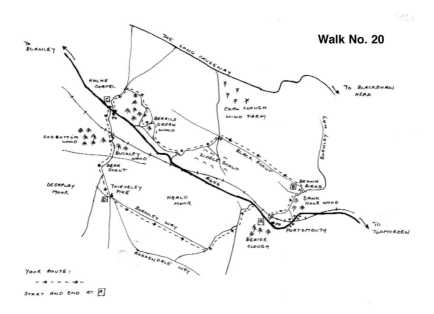

Walk No. 20

101

WALK NO. 20

CLIVIGER'S GORGE-OUS

Portsmouth (GR899263) - Black Scout - Cole Clough - Holme Chapel - Buckley Wood - Thieveley Pike - Heald Moor - Portsmouth

Distance: 8.25 miles (13 km). Leave 4 hours
Conditions: Generally good; very steep section up to Thieveley Pike
Level: Medium - hard

How many times have you driven along the A646 between Portsmouth and Burnley and wished yourself up on either ridge of the Cliviger Gorge and striding along free and invulnerable? And how often have you felt discouraged because you haven't been able to see any walking figures braving it, and felt that it was probably only for the hardy or foolhardy? Dismiss such notions from your mind: you too can share a long but manageable day's walk on those sturdy and ancient cliffs. You're in safe hands especially if you choose a dry day and set out early. Have a friend, a map and a mobile with you to feel confident that you'll stay safe and on schedule.

Cliviger Gorge is the inclusive name for the dramatic terrain embracing Black Scout, Thieveley Scout and Heald Moor, figure-headed at one end by Stoodley Pike and at the other by Pendle Hill and so incorporating both Yorkshire and Lancashire. Its glacial beauty was carved out during the Ice Age by the invincible power of no human and no machine, offering only healed smoothness and leaving no scars: leaving the Gorge's seams of coal and millstone grit exactly where they were.

Either drive or take the 592 bus between Burnley and Halifax to Portsmouth on the A646, and alight near the Roe Buck Inn.

A   Set off from Station Parade, at the western end of Portsmouth, and carefully cross the railway line. Head up the hill on a paved drive and over a stile onto the hillside above Dawk Hole Wood. Aiming to stay above the trees and not descend into the pretty folds of woodland, follow the clear track west of the wood to Brown

Birks Farm. It is quite steep and uneven but it will get you, via a hill-top field or two, to the starting point for your high-ridge walk.

B   Take the marked path to the left of Brown Birks Farm and strike out onto Black Scout. It is a broad, easy path at first. You are walking in the footsteps of ancient wayfarers on a straight route across the ridge - the South Pennines Packhorse Way - giving some fine views down the Gorge, particularly at Riddle Scout - where you should stop and appreciate the views over to the west and take your only chance to grin smugly at the doddery drivers in their cars along the valley floor; you won't see them from this height again on this walk. Your path develops, however, into fields of dense reeds and becomes hard to follow at times. Keep bearing northwest - parallel to the Cole Clough wind farm, and no distance from the Long Causeway (the Mereclough to Blackshaw Head road) to your north. Pass the power station on its left and head down the cloughy, sheep-filled fields to Berrils Green Wood.

The next part is a bit tricky and winding, but bear with it and follow your map closely: traverse the hill towards the woods and climb up behind them, down over a stream, and eventually emerge onto a firm farm track, which leads you down - thankfully, no doubt - back onto the A646 at Holme Chapel where the famous Ram Inn beckons to you from the opposite side of the Burnley Road. (Sup if you will, but it may weaken your legs for the next section!)

C   Cross the A646 and, immediately after the local loos and bus stop, turn left down a small road which will take you under the railway and up into Buckley Wood. This is a pretty, green change of terrain: agricultural and sylvan both at once. Expect yet another quick change, however: the Burnley Way now gives you a sharp, steep climb - very beautiful and exhilarating - onto an open fell and up to the protuberant Dean Scout rocks where you may feel the need to stop and take in the views west beyond Dodbottom Wood to Pendle Hill. Loiter only long enough to feel refreshed to tackle the rest of the stout, steep path up to Thieveley Pike.

D   You are rewarded for your quite taxing climb by only a paltry trig-point surrounded by barbed wire, but also some invisible history and a set of wonderful views. The 'Pike' was an ancient beacon in the northern sequence between Blackstone Edge and Pendle Hill, hence such impelling views over to both. Deerplay Moor lies just beneath you and Bacup beyond it to the south; Burnley, Nelson and Colne hover under grandmotherly Pendle Hill; and on a blue day, even Ingleborough and Pen-y-Ghent come clearly into view.

Go left (southeast) from the Pike, stride along the broad Burnley Way (walking parallel to the Rossendale Way not far to the southwest), across the now threatened Heald Moor which offers you rutted farm tracks underfoot but grand moorlands around you and escarpments beneath you, as well as a home to hardy flocks. Walk for about one kilometre before a shaky, unobtrusive marker points your way left downhill, taking you then onto a rough track - below an unsightly and scoured mining area but with the lovely plantation of Beater Clough and Cock Hill Wood before you - and wind down the 'industrial' tracks to join the A646 once again at Portsmouth.

Refreshments and food for thought await you at the Roe Buck Inn, where I'm sure many and varied opinions on the future of some of the historic terrains you have covered will be served up with your pint - as well, no doubt, as some admiration of your fine walking achievement!

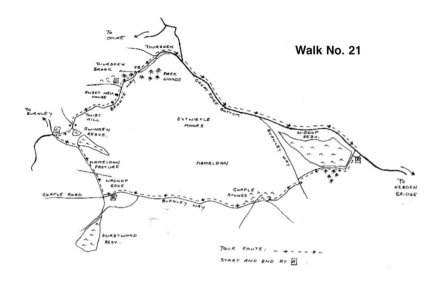

Walk No. 21

WALK NO. 21

LET THE GORPLE GATE FLING WIDE!

*Widdop Reservoir (GR938328) - Gorple Gate - Swinden (Reservoirs) -
Thursden Valley - Great Edge Bottom - Widdop*

Distance: 8.25 miles (13 km). Leave 4 hours
Conditions: Generally good, especially in dry conditions
Level: Medium; two steep ascents

In this land relatively bulging with buses (It is! Take it from an Aussie!), where there is hardly a Yorkshire moor so lonely that a bus doesn't pass it at least once a day, it is indeed odd that one doesn't serve the Widdop Road. Oh, dear, so you may have to succumb to the car - perhaps cycle; or even catch the Blackshaw Head bus, alight at Slack 'junction' and walk the three miles - to your starting point for this walk: the Widdop Reservoir.

And let me also apologise in advance to those who enjoy a pub or two thrown in to these walks, as there is none to be found on this route - unless you give in to the car again and drive to the nearby Packhorse Inn (the Ridge) so that you can still reward yourself with a pint of the local hand-drawn. Otherwise, take your own refreshments and enjoy them en route.

So what has this walk got to commend it? Water, rocks, open moorland, vast vistas, pretty valleys, piercing birdsong and stunning silence, all the monumental magnitude of magnificent Scottish glens and simply knowing that it's all a matter of a few miles from home! It travels where (in spring) the cuckoo calls in the thicket of Widdop pines and rock-climbers clamber up the perilous Cludders Slack. And once over Gorple Gate, the hills tumble away to offer heart-stopping views over Lancashire, and the Great Dame of Pendle makes her entrance to stay with you for the bulk of your journey. And then it drops away into more verdant valleys and burbling streams to bring you gently through woodland, then back at last between the majestic walls of Widdop hills.

And for the children? Try a game of 'I Spy' on a theme of the letter B and I reckon they'll be happily busy the whole of the walk:

Brontë, Burnley, boulders, birds ... just to get you started.

A **From the carpark at Widdop Reservoir, take the main path southwest of the water and, just beyond the plantation, begin the climb up to Gorple Gate.** It is quite a steep climb which intersects with the Burnley Way but which pulls you eagerly to the top. Here stop and take in the glorious views beyond Gorple Upper Reservoir over Worsthorne Moor and Black Hameldon - just fabulous. Carry on along the broad Burnley Way - a safe, firm track - onto 'Gorple Road'. This long, easy stretch takes you beyond the Hurstwood Reservoir 'turn-off' (a strand of the Burnley Way), its pinewoods lying beneath you, and you continue along Gorple Road which would lead you (on another day) east to Worsthorne.

B **Climbing up a short hill and going through a farm gate, you reach yet another 'junction':** two paths cross your track, the left also down to the Reservoir and yours, the right-hand one, taking you over a stile into a rough field at Wasnop Edge, the site of historic but no longer visible remains. Now your 'path' becomes obscured as you wade through the reeds and thistles of Hameldon Pasture. But don't be anxious: just keep bearing left, skirting Wasnop Hill, heading north-northwest, then down to the western corner of the field. (Beware: the surface has been severely holed by cows' feet, and it could be a real ankle-breaker if you don't watch your step.) Farms and reservoir-activity will come comfortingly into view.

C **Drop down to Swinden Reservoirs, which are particularly private and enclosed, but you are most welcome to enjoy the water and wander by their banks.** Then make your way to the top north-western corner of the smaller dam to join the Brontë Way and walk out of the reservoir enclosure via a stile. Skirting the western side of Twist Hill, you will head down into a small, walled valley, then up the hill to Sweet Well House farm. As you emerge onto the farm 'drive', the green patchwork squares of Trawden and Pendle fields, speckled with black and white herds, will bathe the tired moorland eyes. Enjoy the view from the top of a ladder-stile in the wall ahead of you, just before the 'drive' veers away to your left.

D **Here at the top of the hill, you are on stony crags which**

require some care as you drop down to the coppery trees of Park Woods towards Thursden Brook, which will lead you along its banks via a spanking new footbridge to Thursden itself. Follow the path along the riverbed until it meets the Braeside-to-Thursden road. You are back on tarmac for your walk to the Widdop-Colne road 'junction', where it might be wise to pause for refreshment before your robust climb up the hill to Great Edge Bottom.

Enjoy the vista once you reach the top, as the road hems Widdop on its northern edge and affords inspiring Lakeland-like views over the reservoir and beyond - and, hey, you can even see the Pack Horse Inn from here! Hurry along now!

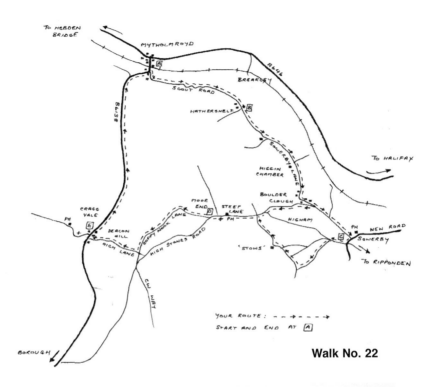

Walk No. 22

WALK NO. 22

THE HIGH ROAD TO STAYING WALKING-FIT IN THE WET SEASON

Mytholmroyd Station (GR012358) - Hathershelf - Boulder Clough - Sowerby - Moor End - Deacon Hill - Cragg Vale - Mytholmroyd

Distance: 7.5 miles (12 km). Leave 4 hours
Conditions: Excellent; just watch for the odd car, farm vehicle or herd of cows hogging the lanes
Level: Medium; two steep ascents

Let me share a little secret with you: I hate walking in the wet. When the rain blows horizontal into my eyes, I just want to cry - and I sometimes do, but usually I think there's quite enough water about without me adding to it. When the boggy mud is up to my knees and my boots feel as if I'm walking on half-thawed crumpets, or it's one ankle-breaking swamp after another and I'm doing more leaping and straddling than walking, then I really am screaming doo-lalley and ready to be carted off to a warm, dry cell.

But there is an answer! Winter walking does not have to be purgatory! Come with me onto the tarmac! When the fogs deign to lift, the views from the ridges are no less fabulous just because you're on the road: in fact, they can be even better. And a tough pair of boots will tackle the tarmac with no more damage to your feet than the slippery hazards of the 'off-road'. We might as well face it: if we want to keep the peaches in our cheeks in winter, on-road it may have to be. And remember, whenever you're feeling a little afternoon blousiness, that's the very time to don those woollies and get out, get up and get heady: out on our welcoming moorland roads.

This walk takes in much of our own fabulous valley and takes you almost as far as the next: the Ryburn Valley - and, for the deal, you'll get charming rurality and stirring moorland tops to admire, all the while being on the delightful winding lanes above Mytholmroyd, Sowerby Bridge and Cragg Vale. Scout Road is your first escort, a lane which only demands a real assault on the energy reserves for the first ascent and some vigilance against its vehicles; then Steep Lane and

110

Coppy Nook Lane take the baton, until Cragg Road (B6138) takes over and brings you home to Mytholmroyd. You will pass the rustic hamlets of Hathershelf and Boulder Clough; you will get views to the northeast over the Luddenden-Booth valleys and, to the southwest, over Soyland and Erringden Moors. And sing out when you see Stoodley - I always do!

A   **Leaving the station at Mytholmroyd, pass south under the railway bridge and turn left into pleasant, leafy Scout Road** for approximately a mile's climb up onto the fine, flat stretch to Hathershelf. Stride exhilarated along the ridge where the views northeast over the fields of Brearley and plateau of Mount Tabor are invariably wonderful, no matter the weather.

B   **Continue along the winding, dipping Scout Road (which continues to test your fitness), past farmhouses and cattle fields.** Past the handsome seventeenth-century farmhouse and cottages at Higgin Chamber on your right, you then drop down into Boulder Clough, with its handsome converted chapel and modest cottages. Make a choice here: either carry on along Scout Road as far as New Road, Sowerby or turn right at Boulder Clough and wind up the sinuous lane to Moor End.

C   **If you take the first option, turn right at New Road, walk up through the village of Sowerby** and, at the junction, bear right, taking the road straight ahead towards the charming weavers' cottages of Higham, heading for Steep Lane and Moor End. (You will pass Stows Weaving Barn at Lower Snape, a warm diversion where you will be amazed at the array of woolly goods on sale and impressed at the large-scale machinery of the small-scale operation.) If you take the second option, the climb is steeper but the distance is shorter and you join Steep Lane just before the chapel on your right. Either way, you will have the steep, narrow hill before you, at the top of which you will pass the newly refurbished Travellers' Rest which may be open at your hours.

D   **Continue up Steep Lane past the turn on your right to Nab End quarries and, at a fork in the road where the hill levels out, bear right off High Stones Road into Coppy Nook Lane.** Walk for a good kilometre along this side-road until you reach a sign on your right for the Calderdale Way - which will lead you down High Lane and past Deacon Hill. Don't forget, before you drop down onto this path, to take in the fabulous views over to Withens Moor and Stoodley Pike (ah!). This shortcut will see you safely down to the Cragg Vale road (B6138).

E **Taking great care of traffic, walking in the cycle lane and watching out for the Cragg village turn-off on the left, saunter down the Cragg Vale hill,** once again taking in the pleasant environment: handsome rows of cottages, farmyards and geese galore. May I suggest that you peel off at Cragg village and take in a pint at the wonderful Hinchliffe Arms (and this time, of course, your boots won't be so muddy that you will have to put the holes in your socks on display!) Then, well watered in hopefully only one way, clamber back onto the homeward road, swing your arms and 'fly' down the hill into Mytholmroyd.

Walk No. 23

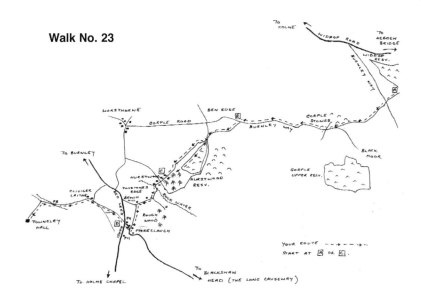

WALK NO. 23

TAKE A TOWNELEY DAY OUT

*Widdop Reservoir (GR938328) to/or **Hurstwood***
Reservoir** (GR883313) - Mereclough - **Towneley Hall, Burnley

Distance:	(from Widdop) 6.5 miles/10 km; (from Hurstwood) 2.5 miles/4 km (one way only). To include time at Towneley Hall, leave 6.5 hours from Widdop; 4 hours from Hurstwood (one way only)
Conditions:	A little muddy in parts but generally excellent: firm underfoot
Level:	Easy (from Hurstwood); medium - hard (from Widdop)

This walk to Towneley Hall, Burnley is totally astonishing. Certainly I had not been so exhilarated by a walk since I was in the South Cairngorms - and this is only li'l ol' Lancashire! Step this way into the Towneley estate and be prepared to be amazed by the beauty and antiquity of this eastern corner of Lancashire.

The walk can start either at Widdop if you're feeling particularly willing or weight-conscious, are prepared to leave betimes (especially in winter, in order to catch the light at the other end of the day) *and* to equip yourself appropriately for a long walk. Certainly it's the more strenuous option, but a family walk from Hurstwood Reservoir will be almost as rewarding (see only sections C - D) - especially since Towneley Hall stands at the end waiting to entrance you, whichever place you start.

For those departing from Widdop, I recommend that you get a lift or a taxi out to Widdop Reservoir, as it will be preferable to leaving the car in a remote spot and give you the additional option of taking the Burnley-Halifax bus home. Hurstwood walkers can safely park the car at the reservoir.

[A   From Widdop, take the main path southwest of the reservoir and, just beyond the plantation, begin the climb across

Rams Clough and up to Gorple Gate. Here stop and take in the glorious views beyond Upper Gorple Reservoir and over Worsthorne Moor, Black Hameldon and Pendle Hill. Carry on along the broad Burnley Way onto 'Gorple Road', the old packhorse route between Worsthorne and Heptonstall.

B   At Ben Edge, at a junction in the ways, go left towards Hurstwood Reservoir. Watch for speeding cyclists on this stretch of the Pennine Bridleway and, as you drop down, you will pass by what look like prehistoric earthworks but which are mere 'sheddings': piles of gritstone discarded and now grassed over. This is where the famous lime industry was once at its height and opened up transport routes from Lancashire into Yorkshire. Walk down to the northern end of the reservoir - still, at the time of writing, at an alarmingly low level and enough to make any soul pray for rain - and, at the edge of the woods where a stile confronts you, choose either to go straight on through the pine trees or to climb up to the right and push your way through high grassland and along the western boundary fence. This latter route offers you wonderful top-of-the-world views over to Pendle Hill.]

C   Either path will take you down into the hamlet of Hurstwood. In this idyllic little backwater, you will want to linger a moment at Hurstwood Hall and try to decipher the stone inscription over the lintel: attesting to its original resident having been a Towneley. Just beyond this fine house sits the elegant beauty of Edmund Spenser's house (the Elizabethan poet of *The Faerie Queen* fame). After you have stilled yourself before these fifteenth-century delights, turn left down the pretty path that takes you to the River Brun (Rock Water) by way of Foxstones Bridge, and make your way up to a group of farmhouses where you turn right onto a farm lane. 200 metres further on at Brown Hill, go left into Round Hill field that skirts Rough Wood and its thought-provoking earthworks. Veer right, through the back garden of a local resident (it is an adopted pathway, so you are permitted through), and then turn right onto the tail-end of the Long Causeway, a few yards from the Mereclough corner.

D   At Mereclough, may I recommend a stop? Choose from either the Kettledrum Inn or the Fighting Cocks. I know which one

I prefer and which is more open than the other but, if you can, I would plump for a cosy nosh here because the Old Stables café at Towneley Hall - despite its pleasant staff and the dubious honour of having been a location for a scene in *Whistle Down the Wind* with Hayley Mills - is less appealing. Once you have supped, cross over Red Lees Road (running between Burnley and Holme Chapel), and take the path into the field directly in front of you, heading for the handsome houses at Cliviger Laithe. From this rise it is a mere step down the hill, crossing the River Calder at the playing fields, and up the 'drive' to Towneley Hall.

This medieval mansion has to be the most successful attraction in our region, for the standard to which it is maintained and the wealth of options it has to offer. On the dank November day I went, I was thoroughly warmed by the welcome from the friendly staff who care as much as if it were their own home. I was mesmerised by the beauty of the Whalley Abbey vestments and the serenity of the chapel. The Parlour hosts many fine art works: especially canvases by Farquharson (you'll recognise his famous 'The Sun had closed the Winter's Day'), Waterhouse, Burne-Jones and Landseer; and the estate also offers a Museum of Local History, a Natural History Centre and an Aquarium.

Extraordinarily, members of the Towneley family maintained continuous residence in this house from the fourteenth century right through till 1902, giving it still a very lived-in atmosphere. Add its deep, mysterious woodlands and its open playing fields and you can only conclude that Burnley must be justly proud of this treasure.

While soaking up all the privileges on hand, don't forget to keep an eye on your watch and start your journey back in good time - either walking back to Widdop, to the car at Hurstwood, or into Burnley town centre to pick up the 592 bus back east.

Walk No. 24

WALK NO. 24

"A WAHNDERFUL SPAHT FOR A PICNIC."

Widdop Road, Walshaw (GR947323) - Walshaw Dean Reservoirs -
*Pennine Way (north, south or east) - **Widdop Road***

Distance: Leave 3 - 5 hours, depending on your choice of route
Conditions: Excellent; both tarmaced and unsurfaced; the
                  Pennine Way flag-stoned in places
Level: Easy - medium, depending on your choice of route

"Ah've fahnd a wahnderful spaht for a picnic" (as Katherine
Hepburn once crackled to Spencer Tracey). Walshaw Dean - a wahnderful spaht which offers perfect peace: lapping water and yapping
curlews, silver skies and otherwise golden silence: perfect as long as
it's not too cold, so pick a day when the sun is at least warming your
face even if the air is crisp, and when the heather-clad hills beckon
you onto the surrounding paths to walk off your sandwiches.

This walk offers you choice: choice of transport, choice of approach
route and choice of post-prandial walking circuit. You can convene at
the starting point either: by car from Hebden Bridge or Todmorden
directions; by bicycle either along the road or across the Pennine
Bridleway from Colden; or on foot (walking or running) from Colden,
or via Hardcastle Crags or Blake Dean. Take a look at your map and
plan your approach from home to the given grid reference.

Once inside the Widdop Road gates (probably locked, but just use
the stile - only tricky when you have to lift your bike over it), you may
cycle, walk or even run in safety - with all the family and even the
elderly - bearing left along the tarmaced 'road', stopping first at The
Lodge to the north of the lower reservoir. Then I recommend heading
for the far northern end of the middle reservoir and picnicking in the
lee of the western wall, just above the burgeoning rhododendron
bushes where it is pleasantly sheltered from the wind. Remember to
put all your litter back into your rucksack and take it away with you.

And whilst champing quietly on your lunch and soaking up the
silence, you can choose your afternoon walk. You can:

1. **go southeast** over the Pennine Way (crossing the reservoir at The Lodge and soon bearing up southeast over Old Dike Hill) to Walshaw hamlet and back to Widdop Road via Blake Dean and Alconden Water (approximately one hour);
2. **head northeast** over the Pennine Way (continuing north along the eastern bank of the reservoir for some 500 metres before climbing over a gate/stile to strike out on the northeastern arm of the Pennine Way) to Top Withens and the Brontë Falls, even to Haworth, and return (approximately three hours);
3. (if you haven't arrived via this route) **go south** via Gorple and Reaps Coppy to May's wonderful Shop at Colden (approximately one hour);
4. **take a leisurely circuit** of the Walshaw Dean Reservoir banks, taking about 50 minutes;

or you could break your party up into pairs, each group setting off on a different route and re-meeting either at The Lodge or the Widdop Road gates after an hour or so. A plethora of choices. "Whaht fun!"

If you take bicycles, I recommend that, for choices 1. and 2. (above), you chain your bicycles to the metal signposts near The Lodge and lower reservoir, and walk. The Pennine Way is a) too rough and steep for many cycles and b) too vulnerable to damage from (fool)hardy mountain cyclists.

You will notice that barely any westerly walking paths exist to or from Walshaw Dean Reservoir and we need to respect some of the 'limitations' which might rankle a little; instead, let's appreciate the range of choices we are still privileged with. Think of it as amazing that such a 'private' area actually offers us quite so many beautiful walks and free access to other routes.

And before setting off back home, no matter whether on Shanks's pony or on wheels, drop in at the Packhorse Inn on the Ridge where the staff will always appreciate your custom, and you can savour some beautifully kept black sheep - as long as you remove your muddy boots.

OTHER BOOKS FROM PENNINE PENS

NATURE'S DOMAIN: ANNE LISTER AND THE LANDSCAPE OF DESIRE
Jill Liddington writes more about Halifax's 19th century lesbian diarist

THE CURIOUS CASE OF DR MANN by Trevor Millum
- disaffected lecturer mysteriously acquires money and seeks revenge

A CANDLE FOR LISA by Debbie Ruskin
- a mother's experience of her baby's death

A VIEW FROM THE BRIDGE
- comic observations from John Morrison, first in Milltown Trilogy
BACK TO THE BRIDGE - second in Milltown Trilogy
A BRIDGE TOO FAR - third

BERRINGDEN BROW by Jill Robinson
40-something woman's search for romance

ANIMAL ANTICS
a collection of children's poems by Debjani Chatterjee.

THE REDLIT BOYS - a collection of poems by William Bedford

EMAIL FROM THE PROVINCES
a collection of poems by Simon Fletcher
NANNY KNOWS BEST - ebook novel from Simon Fletcher
A LITTLE BRIDGE, a collection of poems by Debjani Chatterjee, Basir Kazmi and Simon Fletcher. These three talented Northern poets have collaborated in a collection of poems which reflects the connections between the cultures of Britain and the Indian sub-continent.
THE OCCASIONS OF LOVE
a collection of love poems by Simon Fletcher

THE CHESS BOARD, a play by Basir Kazmi

SYLVIA PLATH: KILLING THE ANGEL IN THE HOUSE (2nd edition) by Elaine Connell, A very readable introduction to the works of this great poet. Elaine Connell also maintains the **Sylvia Plath Forum**
- www.sylviaplathforum.com

ME, MICK AND M31 by Andrew Bibby - Children's environmental mystery

More details of Pennine Pens publications and web design at

www.penninepens.co.uk